Letters to Harvelyn

Phonograph recording of Major Baird's message, read by a Japanese announcer, regarding prisoners of war in Hong Kong, December 17, 1943.

Major Kenneth G. Baird

Letters to Harvelyn

From Japanese POW Camps:
A Canadian Soldier's Letters to His Young Daughter
during World War II

Harvelyn Baird McInnis, ed.

HarperCollins*Publishers*Ltd

*Letters to Harvelyn: From Japanese POW Camps: A Canadian
Soldier's Letters to His Young Daughter during World War II*
Copyright © 2002 by Harvelyn Baird McInnis.

HarperCollins Publishers Ltd.,
55 Avenue Road, Suite 2900,
Toronto, Ontario, Canada M5R 3L2.

www.harpercanada.com

HarperCollins books may be purchased for educational,
business, or sales promotional use.
For information please write:
Special Markets Department,
HarperCollins Canada,
55 Avenue Road, Suite 2900,
Toronto, Ontario, Canada M5R 3L2.

First edition

The newspaper article appearing on page 46 is reproduced with
the permission of The Associated Press. The newspaper articles
on pages 54, 267 and 277 are reproduced with the permission of
The Winnipeg Free Press. The drawings of prison life on pages
59, 65, 66, 78, 154, 193 and 203 are reproduced with the permission of Helen Ballerand and Luba Estes. The newspaper articles
on pages 70 and 74 are reproduced with the permission of The
Canadian Press.

Canadian Cataloguing in Publication Data

Baird, Kenneth G., d. 1957
Letters to Harvelyn : from Japanese POW camps : a Canadian
soldier's letters to his young daughter during World War II ;
Harvelyn Baird McInnis, editor.

ISBN 0-00-200096-2

   1. Baird, Kenneth, 1957—Correspondence.
   2. World War, 1939–1945—Prisoners and prisons, Japanese.
   3. Prisoners of war—Japan—Biography.
   4. Prisoners of war—China—Hong Kong—Biography.
   5. Prisoners of war—Canada—Biography.
   I. McInnis, Harvelyn Baird.
   II. Title.

D805.H85B33 2002   940.54'7252'092   C2002-900562-0

TC 9 8 7 6 5 4 3 2 1

Printed and bound in Canada

Contents

This book is dedicated to all the men of the Winnipeg Grenadiers and the Quebec Royal Rifles. To their wives and children and families who did their best through very uncertain times, to carry on.

To CSM John Osborn, who threw himself on a grenade and died, saving the lives of several Grenadiers. He received a posthumous Victorian Cross.

Ian Adams in *Maclean's* magazine said, "Hong Kong was a disaster, an act of stupidity and folly" that sent inadequately trained and ill-equipped men to defend an island that was indefensible. Too many died in the battle, but nearly the same number died in the camps.

Foreword

Hong Kong Veterans Association of Canada
Patron: H. Clifford Chadderton, CC, O.Ont., CAE, DCL, LLD

This book is based on the diary of Major Kenneth George Baird of the Winnipeg Grenadiers.

He was one of those brave Canadian soldiers who set off to fight the Japanese in far-off Hong Kong, and suffered tragically at the hands of his captors.

We had more than one million men and women who volunteered for service in World War II. It has been my privilege to work on their behalf, but there are four groups in particular who come to mind.

These are the War Amps (of which I am one); the members of the Merchant Navy; the prisoners of war taken in the Dieppe Raid, who were manacled and treated much worse than any other prisoners in the hands of the Germans; and, finally, that tremendous group of men known as the Hong Kong Veterans.

My first contact with the Hong Kong Veterans was at Gordon Head Camp in

Victoria, B.C., where some of them were quartered on their return to Canada, after some 43 months of imprisonment. I shall never forget walking down the aisle between the beds of those survivors who had only recently gotten back to their native Canada. I made my home in Winnipeg before the war and several of the boys yelled out at me because they recognized me from pre-war days. I was in shock when I failed to recognize any of them—such was the ravages upon their faces and in their eyes, wreaked upon them by their inhuman guards in the prison work camps.

I have often said that, of all the groups of veterans on whose behalf I had the privilege to work, none came anywhere near the suffering of the boys who went to Hong Kong. I often wonder, as a good healthy 20-year-old who was in the finest physical condition, how I would have been able to stand the horrors of being a captive of the Japanese. A Japanese soldier adhered to the code of Bushido. Simply, it means that, before surrendering, a good Japanese soldier will fall on his own sword. The idea of this code gave what the Japanese considered as a "right" to treat our Canadian boys with utter disrespect. Any one of them, on a one-to-one basis, could have stood up to the horrible criminals to whom the Japanese Army had given the job of being lord-and-master over these courageous Canadians.

It is to the credit of the Hong Kong survivors that they had the sheer guts, intelligence and belief in the sanctity of the human spirit that allowed them to live through nearly four years of deprivation, cruel and unusual punishment, and slavery.

Cliff Chadderton

Major Kenneth G. Baird

Officers, Winnipeg Grenadiers First Row: *Capt. W. D. E. Morley, Major H. J. Hansell, Major J. L. H. Sutcliffe, Lieut.-Col. O. M. M. Kay, Capt. J. A. Bailie, Capt. G. A. Holman, Lieut. A. V. Dennis.* Second Row: *Capt. E. Hodkinson, Capt. A. R. Gresham, Capt. J. A. Norris, Major G. Trist, Major W. Askey, Capt. J. N. Crawford, Major W. H. Hook, Capt. K. G. Baird, Major H. A. Clarke, Capt. L. T. Tarbath, Capt. A. B. Bowman.* Third Row: *Lieut. J. T. Harper, Lieut. N. O. Bardal, Lieut. A. W. Prendergast, Lieut. R. W. Phillip, Lieut. G. A. Birkell, Lieut. F. N. Symes, Lieut. D. G. Phillip, Lieut. E. R. Anderson, Lieut. J. E. Blackford, Lieut. R. M. Davies.*

"A" Company Headquarters First Row: *Pte. J. Dowie, Sgt. F. E. T. Breakwell, CSM J. R. Osborn, Cpl. R. W. Webster, Pte. A. W. Morgan. Second Row: Pte. L. A. Cardinal, Pte. J. Williams, Pte. G. Lacey, Pte. M. Ambrose, Pte. I. Slipchenko. Third Row: Pte. L. L. Specht, Pte. H. Robinson, Pte. T. Leitch, Pte. R. V. Bennett, Pte. W. T. Carcary. Absent: Pte. R. G. Nutbean, Pte. J. Stephens, Pte. F. Everett, Pte. S. Clark, Pte. A. Clubb, Pte. D. Baxter, Pte. G. Teasdale, Pte. R. J. Brock.*

"B" Company Headquarters First Row: *Pte. G. A. Watts, Pte. J. V. Evans, Cpl. E. C. Wise, CSM W. B. Fryatt, CQMS C. A. McFadyen, Lt.-Cpl. J. Kitkoski, Pte. J. S. Smith.* Second Row: *Pte. H. G. Donnelly, Pte. F. Haufek, Pte. H. Williams, Pte. D. S. Aitken, Pte. W. J. Whitford, Pte. W. J. Smith, Pte. R. J. Turner.* Third Row: *Pte. R. E. A. Larsen, Pte. G. J. Caswill, Pte. G. M. Wilson, Pte. M. E. J. Robidoux, Pte. W. T. Cox, Pte. M. J. Olason, Pte. W. Barrett.* Absent: *Pte. J. Franckiewiez, Pte. N. W. Seymour.*

"C" Company Headquarters First Row: *Pte. J. Miller, Pte. R. Juenke, Pte. J. Eliuk, CSM F. Logan, Cpl. C. J. McArthur, Pte. G. H. Walker, Pte. F. Herc. Second Row: Pte. R. Robinson, Pte. P. M. Williams, Pte. G. Montroy, Pte. T. Dubedat, Pte. W. J. Tuckett, Pte. A. C. Linfield. Absent: CQMS-Cpl. G. S. Ross, Pte. C. Cairns, Pte. R. W. Maybury, Pte. F. A. Harvey, Pte. S. Burden, Pte. J. Hoosha, Pte. F. Fagg, Pte. R. Phillips, Pte. W. J. Cummings.*

"D" Company, Headquarters First Row: *Pte. D. A. Jeffrey, Pte. C. R. Trick, CQMS A. E. Seymour, CSM F. B. Cauldwell, Pte. G .R. Harrison, Pte. W. Smoley, Pte. D. L. Evans.* Second Row: *Pte. P. M. Moysey, Pte. J. W. Leeson, Pte. L. Deslauries, Pte. J. Schreyer, Pte. A. McCorrister, Pte. G.E. Williamson.* Absent: *Pte. O. A. Holden, Pte. R. Dalzell, Pte. D. Hartmeir, Pte. C. Woodhead, Pte. A.C. Carter, Pte. A. G. Carriere, Pte. G. A. Le Gouarguer, Pte. L. Tuck, Pte. R. L. Kirk.*

Inspecting the Winnipeg Grenadiers practising Morse code, from left to right: Major A. W. Hunt, Col. B. O. G. Moton, Brig. Gen. Browne, Lieut.-Col. O. M. M. Kay, and Premier Bracken. March, 1940.

Introduction

On October 25, 1941, the Winnipeg Grenadiers and the Quebec Royal Rifles left for Hong Kong. My father, Major Kenneth George Baird, was one of them.

We had so eagerly awaited Dad's return from Jamaica, where the Grenadiers were training, and were devastated when he was sent off again three weeks later to Hong Kong. We had been told that they were to be posted to Nanaimo, B.C., and Dad had rented a house and bought a car from a friend of his who had been sent to Ottawa.

Three weeks went quickly for Mum and Dad, but seemed a long time to a child of ten. Dad was extremely busy but on several occasions took me to Fort Osborne Barracks where his batman, Bill Fay, taught me to roller skate in the drill hall.

Two weeks after his return from Jamaica, Dad told Mum they would not be going to Nanaimo—that he had been posted overseas. It was the night of the Military Ball and Mum looked so lovely. I wondered why she had been crying just before a nice party, but I was not to know until the day before Dad left.

My grandparents had come down from Brandon to say goodbye and several friends came in that evening. I could hear them laughing and talking and wondered why they were so happy. I felt so sad and alone. Dad left at 5 a.m. the next morning.

When he came in to kiss me goodbye, I was afraid of crying. He had told me to be a big girl and look after Mum. I wanted to say, "Don't go" and "I love you," but knew if I did I would cry, so I said "Have a nice time Daddy," and he cried.

For a ten year old, things are pretty black and white, and life settled down again while we waited for letters to see where he was going. Three weeks later they arrived in Hong Kong and we had a cable and several other letters describing the interesting sights. There was a lot Dad couldn't say, and I, at least, had no idea there might be fighting.

On December 7, 1941, the Japanese attacked Pearl Harbor and Hong Kong. As Dad said, the balloon went up. What a strange thing to say!

Everyone was so completely shocked at Pearl Harbor. December in Winnipeg is cold, but people came out in the streets and stood talking about it. I was with my friend Eleanor Parker on Dorchester Street when one of her neighbours, who knew my mother, came out and said "I guess your Dad is in it now." The next Saturday Eleanor had her eleventh birthday party and Mr. Parker kept patting me on the shoulder. I didn't know why.

It was a very anxious time and we listened to the radio all day, but there was very little news except that the fighting was fierce. When they evacuated from Kowloon to the island of Hong Kong Mum said it was over. I asked if Dad could come home now, but she just hugged me. Usually we went to Brandon for Christmas, but that year we stayed at home, as Mum was afraid of missing any news.

Dad had arranged for his friend, Clifford Midland, to buy me a little radio for Christmas. It was to be, next to my bike, my most treasured possession. On Christmas morning, I unwrapped it, plugged it in, and heard that Hong Kong had surrendered. It was a pretty bleak time for all the families as it was to be many months before we even heard who had survived the battle.

Sometime in the following summer, a man in California picked up a short wave broadcast from Japan. It contained the names of many of the men who were now prisoners of war. It was the first news we had received and we were so grateful to him for sending a small plastic record to the families of each person named.

Sometime after that, the official lists were received in Ottawa, and the sight of a telegraph boy coming down the street struck terror until we saw where he went. Telegrams were never good news.

One day in the spring of 1942, I answered the phone and it was the telegraph operator. Mum was at the bank and the operator refused to give me the message, just a number for Mum to call.

I raced to the bank on my bike and Mum rode it home. The operator told Mum it was bad news and to sit down, and then she read the message.

"Aunt Margaret has died in New York."

Mum started to laugh, and said wasn't that wonderful. The operator thought she had gone mad, but when Mum told her Aunt Margaret was 96 and had been in a coma for several months and that Dad was in Hong Kong, she said she was very thankful she didn't have any other news.

Bill Askey was the regimental Anglican Padre, and he came every week to see us. He was an old friend of Dad's and a source of strength to Mum. He'd knock on the door and say, "Hi Molly—I've come to borrow a glass of sherry." He and his wife were killed in a tragic car accident just after the war ended.

Christmas, Easter, and summer holidays were always spent in Brandon with my grandparents. They were wonderful people and filled a large gap in my life. Every infectious disease I ever had, I had in Brandon. They must have shuddered when we got off the train, wondering what next. In the summer we went to a cottage at Clear Lake. Nana and Mum often went out in the evening to play bridge, and Dada would take me down on the dock, well past my bedtime, and teach me the stars. When we sat out on those starry nights, I'd look up at the sky and wonder if Dad was looking at the same ones. It seemed to bring him closer.

I had been keeping a scrapbook since he left and cut out of the *Winnipeg Free Press* anything to do with Hong Kong. Most of the articles were horrible and made us very anxious as we had heard about the atrocities in Singapore and the Philippines, but life went on.

Rationing came and with it the friendship and kindness of the local Safeway Manager. He had a relative in Hong Kong and saw to it that Mum received an extra tin of jam or can of salmon when these things came in. They weren't rationed but in short supply. Until I was twelve I didn't get any tea or coffee ration, so Mum, a great tea drinker, had to choose. She hadn't had coffee for many months, and when a friend gave her a half pound for Christmas, she cried.

Despite wartime, the Brandon Summer Fair went on. It was a wonderful event, with rides, games of chance, and horse races. We looked forward to it for weeks and talked about it for weeks after. The day after the fair left, all the kids would go to the fairground and look for money in the sawdust on the ground. One year I found eighty-five cents and bought a lot of jawbreakers and jelly babies at Whyte's Pantry.

A friend of Mum and Dad's, George Bond, owned a chocolate factory, and he would come to visit now and again with a five pound box of chocolates for Mum and a one pound slab of chocolate for me. I grew very fond of George Bond and looked forward to his visits! Chocolate was in short supply.

I started taking skating lessons and was in Carnival. My partner, Rosemary Henderson, later joined one of the Ice Shows. She had somewhat more talent than I had!

At school, we had air raid drills and brought twenty-five cents on Fridays for war saving stamps. We pasted them in books and redeemed them after the war. One of the boys told everyone my Dad was in prison because he was bad. He yelled "jailbird" at me every time he saw me and made me cry. Fortunately, the principal, Miss Hallen, heard of it and had a talk with him. He said he was sorry, but I still didn't like him.

From time to time we would receive letters from Dad. Twenty-five words on a card. He often said he was "terribly well," which was something we knew he would never say, so we knew things were not so good. But any news was precious.

On Fridays Mum worked at the Red Cross and I had lunch at Baird's Drugstore. They were very distant relations but not so distant that I didn't get all the broken chocolate Easter bunnies. What a haul!

Mum and the other Grenadier wives saw a lot of each other. They seemed to bolster each other's courage and presented, for the most part, to us, the children, a happy, normal face. We shared birthday parties and church picnics, but under it all was the ever-present fear we could never quite voice. Sheila Young's father was killed at Dieppe. She was a close friend and I think for the first time, I realized that it really could happen.

Gwen Dew, an American reporter caught in Hong Kong and imprisoned there, was repatriated eighteen months later in a prisoner exchange of diplomatic and newspaper people. She wrote a book called *Prisoner of the Japs* in 1943; it was the first real news we had of what had happened there during the battle. Certainly nothing she said eased our fears, but at least it was news and made us feel closer to have some idea of what was going on in the prison camps.

As dreaded as the telegraph boy was, the paperboy yelling "Extra! Extra!" brought everyone out in the street in anticipation. Many people did not have radios—not so much from an economic point of view, but because they were not available in wartime. Which made my own little, brown, Bakelite box very precious. With the "Extras", we read of great battles in the desert, defeats, and successes.

At school, in current events classes, we had maps with flags on pins and moved them forward or backward as the case might be. We had little recent news of our families—most of the letters we received from our fathers were over a year old—and keeping track of the fighting helped encourage us. Many of the children's fathers were in Europe or in England. After June 6, 1944, there were many casualties and often a child would be called out of school, not to return for several days. Very little was said, or encouraged to be said, but we all knew we could be next.

D-Day was so exciting, the paper boys were yelling "Extra" and everyone felt that finally the end might be in sight.

I was finishing Grade 7 in Robert H. Smith school. We had cadets and were warned, "A Slip of the Lip Could Sink a Ship." What secrets they thought we knew, I have yet to discover. We had a club to make money for the Red Cross and to catch spies. A doubtful combination. We, my friends and I, were sure a German family living on the river on Wellington Crescent were spies. We were sure submarines were coming up the river. The fact that they would have had to come from Hudson's Bay was not considered!

News from Hong Kong was scarce and the reports from the Red Cross were not very reassuring. With the Japanese losing in the Pacific we were filled with both hope and fear. Hope that it would soon be over, and fear as to what the Japanese would do.

D-Day on June 6, 1944, was so very encouraging that we lived by the radio and rushed out to buy the "Extras" as they came out. Soon, however, the telegraph boy was seen every day, delivering the news that someone's son, husband or father had lost his life. I have often wondered how those telegraph boys felt delivering such sad news.

During the summer and fall of 1944 we watched the Pathe news on Saturdays at the movies and cheered the advances made by our troops in France and Belgium. We really thought that the war might be over by Christmas and were very upset when the Germans counterattacked in the Ardennes Forest with one of the biggest tank battles in the war. Fortunately, the Germans literally ran out of gas.

In the Pacific, the islands of Guadal Canal and Iwo Jima were being taken by the Americans at great cost and it became evident that Japan would not give in easily.

In the spring of '45, we received three letters from Dad, all nearly a year old. In twenty-five words, he told us he was well and urged us to take a holiday. I had sent him a letter with a lipstick kiss, which he was thrilled to get and wondered if it was his little girl's lipstick, now fourteen, or her mother's?

It was my first one—Revlon Bravo—and I was so proud of it.

V.E. Day arrived in May with the fall of Germany and was wildly celebrated. Japan, we could only hope, would be next.

Japan was now being bombed every day, and we were hopeful that this might bring an end to the war, but fearful that the prison camps might be hit.

In the summer I went out to Vancouver to visit my aunt and uncle, Katie and Wendell Farris. My grandmother was ill in Brandon and Mum went to look after her.

I had a wonderful time in Vancouver and when VJ Day arrived, I celebrated with thousands of others. Aunt Kate took me downtown and I got my first kiss and second, third, fourth, et cetera. It was a fourteen-year-old's dream—all those cute sailors. We hoped Dad would be home shortly and that I could meet him in Vancouver, but he was sent to Manila to hospital for six weeks and didn't arrive home until October 25th. When he did, he had gained sixty pounds and felt fairly well, though he was to enter hospital shortly after with jaundice.

On his recovery, he and Mum took a trip to Quebec for a reunion with the Royal Rifles, and to see my aunt and uncle in Kingston.

Soon after their return, Dad had a massive heart attack and was in Deer Lodge Veterans Hospital for close to nine months. His first heart attack had occurred while on a work party at Kai Tak airport in Hong Kong. After he had been in hospital for some time, the hospital sent my mother a bill for several thousand dollars. Considering that a Major was paid $350 a month, this constituted a lot of money. A friend of my mother's knew the Minister of Health in Ottawa and phoned to tell him that if this hospital bill and all other hospital bills were not rescinded for all ranks for every soldier who was in Hong Kong, she would personally see that every newspaper carried the story. Within twenty-four hours Mum had a telegram to that effect.

After the war, my Dad worked for a while with the Unemployment Insurance office but was never well again. He was weakened from too many years of starvation. The diet the Japanese forced on the POWs led many of them to suffer from diseases caused by malnutrition. My father contracted beriberi and pellagra. Beriberi, a progressive disease that attacks the nerves and muscles is caused by thiamine deficiency. It weakened my father's heart and muscles and led to an early death. He also suffered from pellegra, a shortage of niacin, which can cause skin and facial lesions and can lead to senility or dementia in extreme cases. Like many of the other soldiers interned at Hong Kong, he was afflicted with malaria and dysentery.

My father lived to see me marry and entertained half the Grenadier battalion at my wedding. The day he died, May 8, 1957, he took his two-year-old granddaughter for her first ice cream cone. He was 67 years old, and deserved more time.

The Japanese have never officially apologised for the atrocities they committed, nor have they ever paid any reparations for the slave labour they used.

For many years, the Hong Kong Veterans Association as well as many others tried to rectify this sad situation, but it was not until 1998, 53 years after the end of the war, that the Canadian Government paid $23,000 to each soldier or his spouse. How many do you suppose were still alive?

The Japanese Code name for the attack was HANA-SAKU. The attack had been planned in the summer of 1940, one and one half years before it took place. Three Japanese divisions were thirty miles from Hong Kong when the men left Winnipeg. It was indefensible.

I have a few comments about the editing of this book. In his letters, my father often refers to the Japanese as *Nips* and the Chinese as *Chinamen*. Today we find the term offensive, but during the war it was commonly used and accepted. I have changed the word *Nips* and *Chinamen* to *Japs* and *Chinese*, which I find less offensive by degree.

In the body of the text, I have corrected minor grammatical errors where necessary without comment. Where I have had to change a sentence to make the sense clear or where I have removed text, I have shown these changes with square brackets or ellipses. In places, I have consented to add editorial notes to permit the reader easier comprehension of some of the terms used by my father that have subsequently become obsolete.

Harvelyn Baird McInnis   July 2002

Above, opposite: Winnipeg Grenadiers saying their goodbyes, May–June 1940.

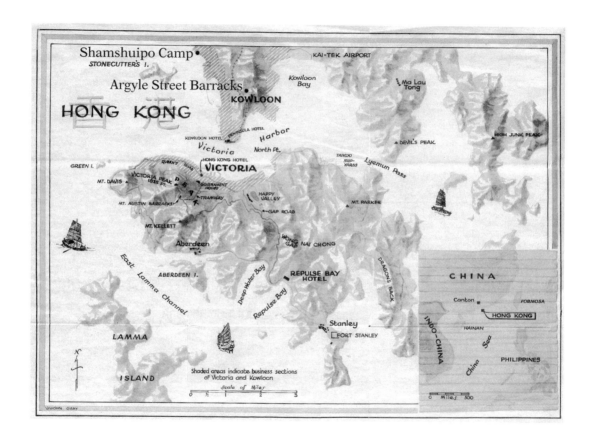

Shamshuipo Camp
STONECUTTER'S I.

Argyle Street Barracks

HONG KONG

香港

KOWLOON

KAI-TEK AIRPORT

Kowloon
Bay

Ma Lau
Tong

HIGH JUNK PEAK

KOWLOON HOTEL • PENINSULA HOTEL

Victoria   Harbor

DEVIL'S PEAK.

North Pt.

GREEN I.

HONG KONG HOTEL
VICTORIA

RUBEN'S 1479

VICTORIA PEAK
1825 FT.

MT. DAVIS

GOVERNMENT
HOUSE

TRAMWAY

MT. AUSTIN BARRACKS

PEAK

MT. KELLETT

Aberdeen

HAPPY
VALLEY

GAP ROAD

TAIKOO
SHIP-
YARDS

Lyemun Pass

MT. PARKER

HONG NAI CHONG

GAP

East Lamma Channel

ABERDEEN I.

Deep Water Bay

REPULSE BAY
HOTEL

Repulse Bay

DRAGON'S BACK

Stanley

FORT STANLEY

LAMMA

ISLAND

Shaded areas indicate business sections
of Victoria and Kowloon

Scale of Miles

0   ½   1   2   3

VAUGHN GRAY

CHINA

Canton   FORMOSA

HONG KONG

INDO-CHINA

HAINAN

China   Sea

PHILIPPINES

0   Miles   500

xxxiv

Letters to Harvelyn

Sunday, August 24, 1941

Dearest Punkle,

It was so wonderful having two such beautiful girls sitting on each side of me at lunch and knowing that they both are the dearest and sweetest in the whole world. You see, dear, I am going to ask you to do me a great big favour, and I know you will too. I would like, sweetheart, to have you help and cheer Mummy in every way. I have to go on a long trip and will miss you both so much, but I know how you will love and comfort Mummy and be such a good girl and study hard, because I know you are the smartest girl in your whole school. I am going to miss you both so much, so please write me often and tell me all that you are doing. Have all the fun you can, and kiss Mummy every day for me.

With all my love,
Daddy

Dearest Molly and Harvelyn,

How I wish a letter would arrive from you two. It has been such a long time since I left—37 days—and it seems like months. We have covered so much territory and ocean and what have you, that it doesn't seem possible that it could be all done in just over five weeks. Since coming here the General CO [Commanding Officer] has reassigned the whole unit. My Coy [Company] has all been split up and for the time being absorbed by the other companies. I am in Battalion Headquarters and as busy as can be, but would rather be in my own Coy with all its worries and little griefs and be twice as busy. We have a peculiar set-up here and until we know just what the Japs are going to do, it will remain as it now is. If the Japs do decide to take a hand in the game, they will find we have a bunch of jokers up our sleeves that will be a headache for them for a long time to come. Last week's show—and it was good—has shown us an awful lot. It was the first time the boys have been in real active service conditions and they worked darn hard and liked it. They returned Friday afternoon.

Friday evening, the Canadian officers were guests at a cocktail party at the H.K. Club. It is a building about four times the size of the Manitoba Club, and is about six stories high. It was a welcoming gesture to give us a chance of meeting the right kind of people, and how they looked after us. They made a point of having one or two members with each officer or group of officers and would keep changing around so they met everyone. Col. Doughty, the Canadian Trade Commissioner here who is from Calgary, was in the 31st Battalion in the last war, and is a great old scout, about 70 years old. He and a naval officer and two other club members looked after George Trist and me. Insisted on us staying at the club for dinner, then took us to a picture show, then to H.K. Hotel for a drink after. It was an awfully nice evening and we landed home about 1:00 a.m.

The club is on the island; we are on the mainland about five miles from there. To get there we take a bus and then a ferry that has to cross the harbour for three-quarters of a mile. I wish you could see the city lit up at night. The whole place is built on the side of a mountain 1,200 to 1,500 feet high, and built up fairly well. In fact, wherever a house can be put, and right on the skyline, are some of the wealthy Chinese homes. There are over 600,000 people in a very small area. When we were going over to the club, we saw a good-sized house on the mountainside in one blaze of light. Hundreds of electric globes all glaring like the dickens. I asked our host later what it was. He said it was a Chinese wedding, and that for the past three nights it had been blazing in lights with hundreds of people out in front singing, playing music and raising hell in general. It goes on for about a week, keeping the whole neighbourhood in an uproar. Their funerals are good too. They have lots of bands, banners, lanterns on the end of long poles and millions of fire-crackers. What a roar goes on when they all play at once, the fire crackers going off hundreds at a time. The crackers scare away the devils that have annoyed the deceased all his life, so that he can go to heaven free from them. One big brass band was jazzing the Dead March the other day with the musicians—if one can call them that—dancing along while playing. It is all very strange. Once in a while, I feel like pinching myself to see if I am really here. I have just asked my Chinese boy to write my name in Chinese. I will try and copy it for you.

K.G. BAIRD  白 奇 志

To get back to the cocktail party, all the Europeans and Canadians and Americans—by Europeans I should have said British people—all their families have been evacuated, mostly to Australia, but many have gone to Vancouver Island, and those who have young families in Canada look upon us as someone from home. A Mr. McKickey and a Mr. Young asked Major Young of the other Canadian Battalion and me to go to their place for dinner one time soon. All these club members are men of darn good positions or they couldn't belong to a snotty club such as that one is. They are frightfully hide-bound in their club rules. As they joked with each other, we got that impression. But they are exceptionally hospitable.

Well, I have to go now.

Best love,
Ken

P.S. Almost midnight. Am just ready to climb into my stony bed. We have been going like the devil since noon, with everyone on their toes, and finished a COs conference at 11:00—we aim to please if anyone wants to start things. I was asked out to dinner tonight with Mr. Porteous, our Auxiliary Services Officer, and YMCA representative to the president of the YMCAs in China. A very swish affair, I am told. All Chinese men and their wives. I couldn't go. It would have been interesting because they put on a dinner one will never forget. I am sorry to miss it. Good night, dears.

[K.]

Wednesday, December 3, 1941

Dearest Molly and Harvelyn,

My letter seems so disjointed. There is so much I could tell you and so little I am allowed to say that it seems I am repeating myself all the time. I got lonely today so I sent you a cable. It goes from here to Singapore, then to Australia, then across the Pacific to Vancouver, then on to you. It was turned in to the Cable Office at 4:00 p.m. on Dec. 3. I wonder how long it takes to reach you. Only three letters have arrived for our boys. They were sent direct. So try yours as follows:

Major K.G. Baird, The Winnipeg Grenadiers, E Battalion, "C" Force, China.

You will get the name of the city off the stamp—via Pan American Airways, San Francisco. Same address, isn't it?

We are hoping for air mail on Saturday or Sunday. I hope it does come, since it seems years since I last saw you and heard from you. I haven't got any idea how our mail is arriving, but I hope it is getting through on time. Am endorsing $10 to get Punkle something for Christmas. Am mailing a parcel when I can get time to do some shopping. I hope it will be soon and the Lord only knows when it will arrive, if ever. Just one present for you today. Hope you like it; will try and get some more this week. We have been terribly busy since arriving, and there doesn't seem to be any let-up, either. I have a new Chinese boy. He is good, too, but makes me nervous. He wants to dress me, but I draw the line at that. He was number one boy for some Col. for years, so I guess he knows his stuff. I am not accustomed to such an efficient valet—darn him. I have sent my 11 cards, or written them tonight, so I am about all-in from such hard work. Am Field Officer on Friday and if a show starts will be really busy looking after the camp here while the others go out. We have a wonderful set-up to meet them, and everyone is hoping something will develop. Good night and best love to you and Punkle. Be sure to look at that fur* if you go to Brandon. I want you to have it, dearest.

Love, Ken

Prison Camp at Kowloon,
Thursday, January 1, 1942

Dearest Molly and Harvelyn,

Trying to outline our trip to date and what may follow from this date onward is a chore that I will find more or less tough. As a narrator, I might make a good lion-tamer—however, here goes.

At 8:00 a.m. on Nov. 16, 1941, we docked at Kowloon, just across the harbour from the city of Victoria, which is situated on the island of Hong Kong. The island of Hong Kong is approximately 14 miles long and about 5 miles wide at the widest point, the terrain is hilly and mountainous, with deep valleys running

* A grey lamb coat, and I did get it!—*Ed.*

in from the sea, the valleys are narrow and well bushed with lots of vines that make progress very hard; later we found this out to our sorrow. Kowloon City, which is on the mainland, forms the southernmost tip of the New Territory; a city of approximately 350,000, it covers an area of about 1.5 miles at the widest point, by about 3 miles long. It is a city of apartment houses, as that is the only possible way the large number of people could be housed in such a small area. There are thousands of small shops, varying in size from a hole in a wall to places about 25 feet square and they always ask three prices for everything.

Kowloon is largely built on reclaimed land that tidewater previously covered. It is, of course, level. The transportation is by buses, taxis or rickshaws, the fares very reasonable. For instance, from our barracks (Hankow and Nanking) to the waterfront, a distance of 4 miles, we would pay 3.5 cents in Canadian money. The city of Victoria, when viewed from the Kowloon side of the harbour, is really a beautiful sight, especially when all the lights are on. The mountains or hills reach a height of about 1,500 feet within a mile of the harbour. They are simply covered with beautiful homes and to see them all lit up at night, it looks like the back curtain in a theatre. One sees these lights hanging in the air—millions of them it seems—right to the topmost peaks.

I wondered how people ever got to their homes, but found out later, as we painfully climbed and crawled over a lot of this ground, after the scrap started. With the exception of a few streets near the waterfront, the city is built on the slopes of these hills and mountains, and the streets are joined for blocks by flights of steps. They seem unending as they go up and down the hills.

Everywhere, the streets are packed with people, quite orderly and going about their business, which seems to be made up mostly of very smelly smells. The sidewalks, lanes, and side streets are filled with little stalls selling anything and everything from girdles to dried grass-hoppers. It is awfully hard to do any shopping as one wanders all over the place looking for a store such as we are accustomed to at home. You will find a store selling dried fish next to a jeweler; he will be next to a fruit seller or a money changer's place of business, and as I only got downtown three times, I didn't get acquainted with the city at all.

From Nov. 16 to Dec. 8, our battalion was occupied from early morning until evening on training, which we woefully needed. The company commanders were continuously on reconnaissance of the island defenses. The mainland had its first line of defense at the frontier, 25 miles away, defended by the Royal Scots and the Middlesex Regts., the Royal Artillery and Indian Artillery. They were supposed to occupy impregnable positions but lasted about three days and retreated in the face of superior numbers and arms. This is a most elementary outline of our first three weeks after our arrival, but believe me we were busy day and night trying to solve our problems.

Then the morning of December 8, 1941, arrived and as the Imperial troops loved to say, "The Balloon went up." How I got to hate that expression. It is one of two expressions the Powers That Were loved to use and they were both so damned futile. Whoever coined these phrases, I am sure felt he had done his bit in this campaign and retired to an easy chair in the Battle Box 80 feet below ground and peacefully slept for the duration.

The first we knew that war had begun was when the Japs came over and bombed us on the morning of Dec. 8, about 8:00 a.m. Bombs are not conducive to peace of mind, especially the first ones dropped; one's mind starts functioning at an extraordinary rate, while one remains perfectly still in his tracks and wonders just where they will land. We weren't left long waiting. The first lot of bombs landed about 200 feet away from where we were standing. Between shrapnel, stones, broken glass, and plaster, which didn't add to one's comfort or peace of mind, our attempts of acting indifferent and trying to be nonchalant were, I am afraid, not quite successful. Their first trip killed six men, fortunately not of our unit, and wounded about 20 others, some of whom were our troops.

These men had been quartered in the Jubilee Building. Our battalion had gone into their positions on the island of Hong Kong on Sunday, Dec. 7. My company, plus Capt. Norris, our quartermaster, and his staff, and our Officers' Mess staff were left in Hankow Barracks with orders to proceed to our positions on Monday, the eighth. A ferry had been ordered to call for us at 9:00 a.m. It was late and when it finally arrived I lost no time in getting my company aboard. They of course sent a small tug and we were packed on like sardines. We went to the island, landing at the Royal Army Service Dock about five miles away. Why they didn't bomb us I don't know, as they were playing hell all over the place. We had left our barracks with everything we owned locked in our rooms. All we could take was one haversack with a few necessities. Fortunately our things were brought over by Capt. Norris and his staff during that day and night of the eighth. They were piled anywhere and everywhere at Wan Chai Gap where our Battalion HQ was situated. I am afraid there will be quite a lot of "I" in this, but as it is only meant for you, Molly, and Harvelyn, and as it only deals with the very small part I played in the show, I am afraid the "Is" will have to be excused.

I took my company to Wong Nai Chong Gap where the Canadian Brigade Headquarters were situated. This gap is on the main cross-island road, and a place where later our men put up such a gallant fight against numbers at least 10 to 1, and where so many of our officers and men were killed or wounded, and where Brigadier Lawson and Brigade-Major Linden were killed. I was then sent on through to Stanley Gap to the huts and dugouts of Stanley and Tytam Gaps. This position was on our extreme right flank and one of the bleakest parts of the island. There was about a mile on our right not protected before the positions occupied by the Royal Rifles of Canada were reached. We stayed there two and a half days and two nights. We were on the *qui vive* all the time and I don't think we had more than two hours sleep in each twenty-four. On the third day we were ordered back to Wong Nai Chong Gap where we found that Capt. Bowman and his Company, "D" Coy, had been sent back to the mainland to help bolster the line that was being pushed back—our first line of defense. We were at Wong Nai Chong from the afternoon of the 11th until the early morning of the 14th; during this time sleep was a luxury few indulged in. Oh, while at Stanley Gap, the colonel came over and found me wrapped up in a blanket shivering and sneezing and with a temperature. He insisted on taking me back to HQ. The cold I had in the Robinson Bldg. had been gradually taking hold of me and finally caught up. I had gone to bed the Sunday before (the seventh) feeling darned homesick and wanting you to make a fuss over me and then having to get going on the morning of the eighth and keep it up. Well, to make this part short and snappy I landed at a dressing station (first aid post). Lieutenant Colonel Sutcliffe didn't think I looked so spry and wanted me to go to the hospital. I spent the night in the dressing station where they filled me up with stuff and nonsense, and at 6:00 a.m. the next morning they said my temperature was normal, so I beat it before they could say or do anything else to me. My voice had deserted me and it really was funny to hear me croak. I got back to my company that morning of the 10th, so was only away overnight.

That night, when I was on duty and trying to keep awake, I decided to write you a letter. I have it in front of me now. It is a masterpiece of disjointed literature. I must have dozed about every other line, because it is hard to make sense of it. One thing I really worried about was you and Harvelyn, Molly, because I know how you were worrying and right now, the 26th of June, over six months after our capture, I don't think you know how we are. I pictured our home and you and Punkle there. I loved it and knew that nobody but you could make it as beautiful as it is. I thought of Harvelyn skating and going to her little parties; she had several friends who had birthday parties during Nov. and Dec. I seemed to remember, and hoped she would have a lovely time, while I knew you would be worried sick but still smiling. Yours is the hard part, dearest, I know. This letter I am looking at says I am going to waken one of the officers at 2:00 a.m. and I have decided to call the one that is making the night hideous with his snores. He reaches high C one moment then comes out with some blood-curdling low notes that are nearly unbearable. Yes, I woke him up and crawled on to the concrete floor for a little nap.

When we arrived at Wong Nai Chong Gap where Brigade Headquarters were established, we really started to get busy. We had only a handful of men to man all the posts in that area and were going night and day. Everyone was as tense and keyed up as possible as this gap was the one way the Japs could cross the island from north to south and divide our forces—which they later did. My officers and I were kept jumping, putting in roadblocks, manning machine gun posts, wiring the dugouts and a hundred other things, such as patrols, etc. The bane of my life was the telephone—the darn thing seemed to ring incessantly. Between answering it and running over to see what the brigadier wanted and had in mind, and I found he had plenty, what with slim rations and practically no sleep, you can just imagine how sweet our tempers and dispositions were. Yet up to that time in comparison to what followed during the next 11 or 12 days we were having quite a little picnic and didn't know it, because we hadn't contacted the enemy at close quarters. After all, things are only great or small, hard or easy, pleasant or unpleasant, by comparison.

During the night of the 13th/14th, we arrived at Wan Chai Gap. Capt. Bowman had returned and relieved my Coy. That was the last time I saw him; he was killed about the 19th or 20th, and never found by anyone. Wan Chai, our Battalion HQ, is immediately above the eastern part of the city of Victoria on H.K. Island overlooking the naval yards and ordnance stores. This we found out later, as it was as black as the inside of a tar drum when we came over the road in buses and trucks without lights, and why we didn't land in the middle of the city hundreds of feet below, speaks well of our drivers' ability to see in the dark. My eyes seemed to be popping trying to see. It is a trip not prescribed by nerve specialists for their patients. We arrived about 3:00 a.m. and I got my men settled for the night and then reported to Col. Sutcliffe. I found him up to his eyes in work and trying to answer three phones at once and doing a real man's work. After making my report and asking for orders, he sent me up to the mess at 530 Coombes Road, just near our Battalion HQ. This house was someone's beautiful home. I had hot coffee. No, a good slug of rum first—straight—that we had brought all the way from Jamaica. It left me gasping for a while but warmed me up and gave me enough pep to drink some coffee and eat a sandwich. I felt there could be nothing so good as a night's sleep, but discovered that it was after 4:00 a.m. and stand-to at 5:30 only a little while off, so I wrapped a ground sheet around my shoulders and went outside. It was still dark, with daylight not far off. Stand-to was from

5:30 a.m. until half an hour after broad daylight. This is always an eerie time; I think we all have inherited from the Dark Ages a certain amount of fear of the dark. I know things seen in daylight have an entirely different effect on one's mind and actions. In the light we can see, judge and decide what seems best to do, be it right or wrong, while at night we have to go by instinct. And in addition we have that feeling that darkness contributes—a sense of insecurity.

When daylight came on the morning of the 14th and we were able to see the sort of country we were in, we were surprised to find ourselves in the midst of a small town made up of beautiful homes. These homes would cost from $10,000 to $75,000. They had all, with the exception of three or four, been deserted. Our men, along with other units, were billeted in these homes. I took 50 men into the drawing room at 555 Cameron Road and bedded them down for the night amid surroundings, which I am sure, few or any of them had ever seen before. This was the American consul's home; his family reserved a few rooms in the back of the house. Our mess at 530 Coombes Road was selected because it was close to the central dugouts where every part of our defense system on the island was linked by phone. I had my company office in a huge house—528 Coombes Road.

The second day there, the Japs put a 6-inch shell in one of the rooms killing six men and wounding several more. It was not very pleasant getting them out. The door was filled up and we had to tear our way in through one of the heavily shut-tered windows and bring the men out on doors or anything else we could find. We soon had them on their way to the hospital. I didn't get any sleep on the 14th and neither did the others, and looked forward to evening when I felt sure a little could be had. About 4:00 p.m., Col. Sutcliffe sent for me and said it was up to my com-pany to take over the defense of Wan Chai Gap. I felt as though I had been handed a hot iron with no place to put it, so I made a thorough reconnaissance and found the place could easily be attacked from three sides. I had to spread my Coy over a large frontage as the Japs could come in from the north, east, and south: the north, or city side; the east, Mount Cameron; and south, up from the east side of the island through Aberdeen. The south and east were covered partially by two other companies and further west by the Hong Kong Volunteers and some of the Middlesex Regt. Mount Cameron due east and right above us, about 800 feet high, was a perfect spot to strafe us from, with trench mortars and machine guns. We had a machine gun post up there, a hell of a climb to get there and back, and doing it at night in the dark and rain was about all anyone could stand. For the next six days and nights it seemed that all we did was string barbed wire by day through the bush and trees around Battalion HQ, and fill sand bags by night, then place them in positions that would afford the most cover for the few men we had manning the many posts that covered the approaches to the Wan Chai Gap. I have forgotten in which war the thin red line was mentioned, but it was densely populated in comparison to ours. When one has less than 100 men to cover a frontage of two and a half miles as "B" Coy had, and "A" and "C" Coys weren't any better off, that feeling about the dark has some grounds for existing.

On the morning of the 19th I had my first close call. I had been shaving at our mess—530 Coombes Road—I had just finished and was drying my face and Capt. Terry, our paymaster, was bending over the basin washing, when a shell hit the top of the window. It completely ruined the bathroom, wounding Capt. Terry in several places down the back. The explosion sent me 15 feet end-over-end into the corner of the next room. (I'd been standing in the open door talking to him.) I landed on top of a big box and rolled into the corner. I sailed through the air with the greatest of ease but landed damn hard. I went back and dragged Capt. Terry out. He was semi-conscious. I got him into the dining rooms where about 10 of the officers were having breakfast. They knew, of course, the house had been hit but didn't know where. They sent for the ambulance and took him off in a hurry. I got three hours' sleep that day and averaged not more than that for the 18 days of the war. Everyone carried on with little or no sleep—sometimes for 48 to 60 hours at a stretch—then they would simply pass into sound sleep on their feet.

This was caused by the pitifully small number of men we had. They tried to do the work and cover the ground that five times our numbers were needed to do.

On the afternoon of the 19th it started to rain and blow. The troops left at HQ took up a position on Mount Cameron about 1,500 feet above sea level. They had about 1,000 yards of frontage. We had about 30 Royal Engineers on our right flank. They pulled out just about 7:00, just after dark, and left our right flank wide open. Their Col., a perfect wet smack and bag of wind, was very annoyed and put out when I caught these blighters coming back to their billets and ordered them back. I then went to HQ and found Col. Sutcliffe, the Engineers' Col. and two other colonels there and reported the whole thing; Lordy but the blighter was mad! If I hadn't been so darn tired and mad I wouldn't have said all I did but I called the men and their officer that brought them out all the yellow blinkety blanks until Col. Sutcliffe told me to go easy. Their Col. said his men had been on for 12 hours and were tired, cold and hungry. Ours had been up there in that gale and wet for nearly 36 without any hot food or drink at all, and had been doing just that since the eighth. We felt the scrap was a serious thing, while the Imperial troops, or most of them, seemed to be trying to think up new excuses for not doing or trying to do the obvious things that had to and should have been done.

RECOMPENSE
(In memory of a bayonet charge, 19 Dec.1941)

Machine guns sow the slope with death
In angry bursts which spell defeat,
And blasted by that hateful breath,
They fall as hail cuts down the wheat.

Still stubbornly they press the strife,
For well they know our cause is just
They fight for things more dear than life
The rights of men are in their trust.

Up, inch by bitter inch, they toil
For die they may but win they must;
Now from the steel their foes recoil,
Butt stroke, parry, thrust.

And, suddenly, they've won the ground,
A transient triumph all too fleet
But glory has no hollow sound;
That charge, with victory replete
Became their leaven seldom found
In bitter bread of dark defeat.

Composition by an unidentified soldier, collected in a hand-made booklet entitled "Hong Kong Hodge Podge," Christmas, 1942.

20

"A," "B" and "C" Companies were on the south side of the island catching merry hell from all angles, and trying to keep back five times their numbers. Fortunately, on the 20th, the Japs withdrew from the east side of Mount Cameron and gave our men a chance to get some proper food and some rest. As I said before, I had the Wan Chai Gap area and had six guards and road blocks that I had to visit during the night, besides looking after the crew of about 80 men filling sandbags and carrying them to the places we were trying to strengthen: shelters, sentry posts, etc. How those boys worked! Even though they could hardly stand from tiredness. Yet we had a lot of yellow bums that left their posts and sneaked back to their billets. Some of them even left the food and hot tea for the men on Mount Cameron and beat it to God knows where. Our sandbag party would stop work about 3:00 a.m. and go back to their billets for a couple of hours sleep. That night it rained so hard I had about two hours' sleep. I was soaked from the waist down; I went to the Mess, had a drink, and the only place I could find [to sleep] was under the table, so I crawled in there and in about two minutes was awakened—or it only seemed that long —for stand-to at 5:30. All day long of the 20th we were going like mad.

The morning of the 21st was at least dry, and about 8:00 a.m. the shelling began, also bombing. They had 15 or 18 heavy bombers, and all their lighter planes laid eggs also. They had over 50 planes—we hadn't even one—so they did just as they pleased, and so our day began. Our movements had to be as guarded and concealed as possible during daylight hours, and we were always being driven to cover by snipers, who seemed to be awfully close, and the ping of a bullet going by kept us moving all the time. About this time, the Powers That Be were beginning to wonder what it was all about, and what a flop they were. It really was pitiful, the chaos that filled them all at Battle Headquarters. Orders given and countermanded several times during an hour or two's time, and then to try to square themselves, they would order an attack with men so tired . . . they could hardly stand. They could never give us any information of the enemy and would accept none from us. Things we could easily see they said were wrong, or were our own troops or ships when we hadn't a ship of any kind afloat. I suppose our losses were about 25 per cent. This was our daily "diet" for the last three days of the scrap.

Christmas Eve arrived with everyone fairly exhausted, and the Japs piling troops by the thousand on the island. We could see them bringing them over from the mainland in ferries and reported it but could do damn all about it. All our big guns were placed to shoot out to sea and as the Japs knew this, they came over where only a few of our guns could reach them. At best we had only a handful of guns and most of them were useless as far as reaching the spots where the fighting took place.

On the night of the 23rd of December I managed to get a few of my Christmas presents out of my box, but had to leave before getting them all, and since have lost everything I had. I wish I could have gotten away with my things, especially all my clothes—hundreds of dollars worth—but then if I had taken them from where I had them I couldn't have carried them very far. I could have changed into my uniform (serge) and taken some shirts and socks and underwear, but then it would have been darn hard deciding what to take and what to leave. Note: in this I seem to jump back and forward from day to day but the notes I have to write this from were written after we went to Shamshuipo, so if they seem all jumbled up it is just too bad.

On the night of the 21st/22nd we had orders to withdraw the whole line from Mount Cameron and go back to Mount Gough. There had been hell popping all day all along our front. The Japs broke through on our right flank; our wounded, those that could walk, hobbled out; some were carried. Mount Cameron was evacuated about 10:30 p.m. and our men started coming off the mountain. It was awfully dark and getting the wounded down the hills through the rocks and bush gave the men really something to do. I had the odd truck there to take the wounded away in. I got word that Capt. Prendergast was badly wounded and sent two men back for a stretcher. A number of my men came tearing back with the stretcher and thought it was I that had been wounded; however, Alex only had a slight wound and got out under his own steam to where the dressing station was. I was surprised to see the number of women and children that came from the houses. Babies and youngsters like Harvelyn. Believe me, I was glad you and Punkle were in Winnipeg. We fired our ammunition supplies and what a roar they made. Firecrackers by the thousand would be nothing to the noise it made. My Coy brought up the rear party and we started for Mount Gough. Everyone was dead on their feet and when you start on a three-mile march all uphill, carrying everything you have left in the world (which wasn't much, but seemed to weigh a ton), trying to find a place we had never been to or even seen . . .

A guide was to have been left for my party. He wasn't there and we took the wrong road and had to come back. That half-mile extra nearly broke the camel's back. When we finally got on the right road and were told we had another two miles to go—it was at least a definite objective to reach—there were many with minor wounds carrying their rifles and Bren guns that the rest of us tried to spell off for a little way, but they insisted on taking them back and doing their own bit. About 2:00 a.m. we arrived at our destination and we all sat down just where we were on the roadside and rested until we were told to hunt cover, because it was then starting to get light. I took my Coy into Ho Tung's garden; he is or was a very wealthy man, and his place must have been nice at one time but was fairly badly blown about. We had to take shelter under the trees and bushes and weeds on the side hill—there seems to be nothing but side hills all over the damned island—and the people living above had made a dumping place for all their old tins, bottles, bricks and anything else they had to toss away. This is what we had to sit or lie on. Very few got any sleep. We were very close to a battery that annoyed the planes as they came over, so we had picked a warm corner to spend the day. They bombed the Indian Battery that were quartered right in front of us, and what a shambles they made of them.

Men and mules by the dozen, big homes on fire, ammunition dumps exploding, and we had ringside seats. We were protected from view by the trees, but oh boy! it didn't seem to give one much cover. The bombs would go near our heads and hit about 200 yards away—tough on the other fellows, though. About 2:00 p.m. on Dec. 22, we were ordered to make a reconnaissance of the far slope of Mount Gough. Major Hook ("B" Coy), Capt. Bardal ("A" Coy), and I went to look over the ground and found it nothing but a death trap as it could be seen from three sides. After doing this and reporting back to Battalion HQ that the place was untenable, we received orders to go back to Wan Chai Gap and take up positions along Mount Cameron again. This was really the beginning of the end. Major Hook with "B" Coy took up his position from the base of Mount Cameron with Capt. Bardal on his right. They were to link up with Major Bailie at Aberdeen. My company took up the top of the ridge from Magazine Gap to Wan Chai Gap covering the approaches from Mount Cameron and Stubbs Road and Black Links Road. I had my company in four houses along the top of the ridge where we had a good field of fire. We cleaned up on a good number of Japs that had M.G. [machine gun] and mortar positions on the north slope of Mount Cameron, about 650 yards away. Lt. Hennessey, an Air Force officer that came to us and helped out, along with Sgt. Faulconer and Cpl. Darragh and his Vickers-gun crew, really went to town on the 24th and cleaned up the two posts mentioned above. We were shelled heavily that afternoon and on Christmas morning business really opened up with a bang. They drove two of our parties out of their houses by machine gun, trench mortars and artillery shells and then started bombing. I brought the officers and men from these houses back to where I was, and sent some to the house that Vic Dennis was in charge of. As the day progressed we were being continuously sniped at every time we had to go out—which seemed too often altogether—as we had to keep in touch with our other platoons and get reports from them to send to Battalion HQ.

N.S. 1320b A.F.C. 2128 R.A.F. 96 Nat. Def. B. 305 140M Pads 100—9-39 H.Q. 1772—39-428	**MESSAGE FORM**		Serial No.	

CALL AND INSTRUC- TIONS	IN	No. of Groups GR.	OFFICE DATE STAMP
	OUT		

TO   Baird

(ABOVE THIS LINE IS FOR SIGNALS USE ONLY)

FROM   Sutcliffe

Originator's Number	Date	In Reply to Number

Yes. Do as you suggest and also watch out for
their details coming from Tough Hill. They
have orders to stop just the other side of
Magazine Gap and await orders. Take charge
of them and hold them in Reserve on
Thoomby Road just below Your Headquarters.
See to that while I take up Your dispositions

THIS MESSAGE MAY BE SENT AS WRITTEN BY ANY MEANS	IF LIABLE TO BE INTERCEPTED OR FALL INTO ENEMY HANDS, THIS MESSAGE MUST BE SENT **IN CIPHER**	ORIGINATOR'S INSTRUCTIONS DEGREE OF PRIORITY	TIME OF ORIGIN
SIGNED Sutcliffe	SIGNED		**T.H.I.**

(BELOW THIS LINE IS FOR SIGNALS USE ONLY)

SYSTEM IN	TIME IN	READER	SENDER	SYSTEM OUT	TIME OUT	READER	SENDER	SYSTEM OUT	TIME OUT	READER	SENDER	
												T.O.R.

Message from Col. Sutcliffe to Major Baird, regarding Magazine Gap.

27

Major Baird's message to Lt. Dennis, and Lt. Dennis' response.

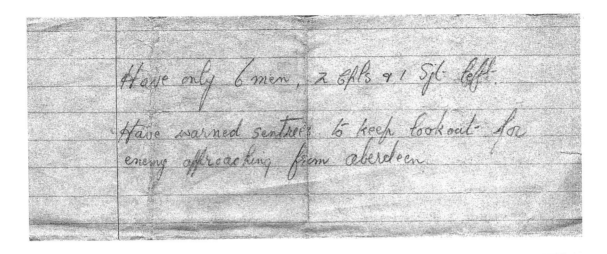

Have only 6 men, 2 Cpls & 1 Sjt. left.

Have warned sentries to keep lookout for enemy approaching from aberdeen.

The men carrying messages did some fast work in getting over ground from one bit of cover to the next, and most were lucky.

From 11:00 a.m. until we had to evacuate at 4:00 p.m. (Xmas day), the house I had my Coy Headquarters in simply bounced and danced all over the place. If it hadn't been for exceptionally thick foundations made of cut stone over two and a half feet thick, with reinforced concrete and thick brick walls dividing the basement up into many rooms—there must have been 12 or 15 rooms in the basement—if it hadn't been for these protecting walls, we all would have been buried under tons of stone, etc. I didn't think it possible that a building could take so much punishment and still stand up and stay together. There must have been 30 or 40 bombs that hit in the immediate vicinity of that place. The noise was deafening, of course, and the ones that hit the house shook our livers more than riding horseback ever could do.

At 4:00 p.m. I received orders to evacuate our positions and fall back beyond Mount Gough with Headquarters at the police station where we had been on the night of Dec. 21/22. How they plastered Magazine Gap, where we had been since the evening of the 23rd. Our trip back to Mount Gough was hot and tiring, with nearly everyone dead on their feet from long hours, little food, and no sleep and under fire most of the way. As we drew near the Peak and our destination, we were told that an armistice had been signed; we were ordered to turn our arms and ammunition in. We put ours in a pile along with other troops in the yard of the Peak Mansions, a beautiful apartment house that was badly torn by shellfire. I then proceeded on my way towards the Mount Gough Police Stn. where we were to rendezvous. Just before arriving there I met Col. Sutcliffe and several of the other officers coming towards me with about half of our battalion. We were just near a big ammunition dump that was on fire, and the big shells and small shells started to explode. All hell seemed let loose, so we got past it in one heck of a hurry and around a bend in the road where things were more peaceful. We stopped and Col. Sutcliffe spoke to everyone for a few minutes. It was then about dark so we started for Mount Austin Barracks, where we spent the night. We were all in. Some rations came up consisting of bully beef and hardtack biscuits—and I mean *hard*—and a tin of fruit that had been scrounged from the N.A.A.F.I. [Navy, Army, and Air Force Institutes] store. We then started looking for a place to sleep. The Col., the adjutant and I slept in the quarters that had [housed] the commandant of the barracks. Plaster and bits of wall over everything. I slept on a Chesterfield with some velour hangings for covers and really slept. The next day we all were assigned quarters for our companies by the Col. and started getting them cleaned up and in some sort of livable shape. It is there that Ross Davies is buried (Mount Austin Barracks). I found his grave just outside the building where we were quartered. He was killed by concussion, I heard. Also, Col. Hennessey was badly wounded by the same shell. He died the next day—two darn fine men. Our men worked like the devil all day long, moving tons of debris. And when night arrived we turned in about 9:00 p.m. At 10:00 p.m. we were ordered to fall in as we had to move to some other place. You can imagine how everyone felt—we were all fit to be tied—but move we did, down to the Peak

Mansions. This was on the night of the 26th. We put our men in two or three suites of about 12 rooms each, all beautifully furnished, that the people had just walked out of, leaving all their clothes, silver, furniture, etc., as it was, with well-stocked larders and wine closets. We had to do some quick moving to gather up the liquor. I was wishing I could transport it home by thought wave—dozens of bottles of the best liqueurs and wines of every kind. We each had a good snort before turning in.

The next morning, soon after we had had our breakfast, we were told we were going to be moved again. We were thoroughly disgusted over this new order: we thought we had found a happy home. We packed as much canned goods as we could carry with us, in addition to our scanty supply of clothes. The night we spent in Peak Mansions was the first time I had been undressed in over 10 days and how good it felt. The morning of the 27th we moved off from the Peak Mansions for some other place. Where we were being taken we had no idea, and cared less. You remember the pictures we used to see of refugees trekking along in a long line, looking as despondent and woebegone as possible? Well, that was our party true to life—we had over 1,000 Indian troops along with us and they are the scruffiest, dirtiest lot I have ever seen. We walked for over two hours, with only one halt for rest, carrying about 80 or 90 pounds of clothes, food, etc. Fortunately, it was all down the side of the mountain—the "Peak," the highest on the island at nearly 2,000 ft.—following paths and narrow roads. The troops and officers were clothed in anything they could get their hands on for warmth, it was so darned chilly. Finally we landed at the University of Hong Kong and were told to sit down on the lawn. We didn't have to be urged, either. None of us had had any water for over 24 hours and were feeling it by that time. I took my water bottle and went up to one of the guards, a flat-faced Jap, and went through sign motions trying to make him understand we needed water. He gave me a push and pointed to where I had been sitting, and gave me to understand to get the hell over where I should be. After several attempts to get other guards to let me go, and having spotted a water cart down the road below where we were, I collected about a dozen bottles and walked by the blighter, and kept on going. He yelled at me a couple of times but I didn't think he would shoot, and my guess was right. From then on I was the only one he would let go, so I played Gunga Din for about an hour and a half.

All that day, the CO and the officer in charge of the Indian troops were trying to find out where we were to stay for the night. We were then ordered to go back up to the Peak Mansions. We were ready to murder the lot of them by that time as I am sure we couldn't have climbed those hills without some food and a good rest.

They kept on arguing about it so long that it started to get dark and they decided to let us stay the night where we were. They gave us some tinned bully and biscuits, and we had brought along the odd bottle of scotch so we curled up on the floor of the balcony of the Auditorium (the officers) and got some sleep. The floor was quite soft. That night my wardrobe consisted of one pair of shoes, three pair socks; one uniform, battle dress; one sweater, one wedge cap, four shirts, two pair K.D. [Khaki Drill] shorts, two suits of underwear, and about a dozen hankies. As I hadn't taken my clothes off for the past 10 days my trousers looked as though I was perpetually ready to make a big jump at any second, they were so baggy. We found breastworks all around the university buildings, built of bags of flour instead of sand. It seemed darn funny to be as hungry as hell, and to find out that one of the buildings about 100 yards away was an A.S.C. store house, bulging with all kinds of good things to eat and the Japs wouldn't let us anywhere near it.* The British had enough canned goods and biscuits to last their troops for two or three years, besides huge food stores for the civilian public. The Japs have now, at the time I am writing, July 10th, moved nearly all of it away.

The morning of the 28th we were told we were going to move again. Luckily the

* An A.S.C. store house is a British supply depot.—*Ed*.

Japs brought a big carton into the room where we were, filled with silverware: knives, forks, spoons of all sizes—all sterling silver, and most of it crested—that they had gathered up some place, so most of us got our eating utensils then and there. I still have mine and guard them carefully. Our water supply was exhausted and we only had enough water bottles to give one to every four men, but that helped a lot. There were a few instances where we would have been perfectly justified in shooting a few of our men for their conduct, but I won't put the details on paper or mention their names. At 10:30 on the morning of the 28th we were ordered to move on once more. It certainly seemed that nobody loved us. We were still feeling quite sorry for ourselves and hated another long march; however, we left and finally landed at Victoria Barracks in the heart of the city, right near the China Command Headquarters. These barracks had been quite new and really wonderfully built of reinforced concrete, but had been shelled very heavily and were a general shambles. We all worked for two days cleaning up and getting supplies of food together. Six of us slept on the floor of one little room. We were all busy getting the companies sorted out and re-organized and allotted to quarters. We ate out of cans, as we had no plates and were just beginning to see daylight, when we were told we were going to be moved on the morning of the 30th. We fed our men at 5:30 a.m. and had our breakfast of beans and bully beef, some cheese and crackers, and tea. We then packed all the rations we had in bags, and distributed them through the unit to be carried to our next stop. We were feeling all in, because everyone had worked like the devil cleaning up the various places we had stopped in, and when I say we moved hundreds of tons of debris, I mean just that. We started at 7:30, loaded down with our worldly possessions plus what food we could carry. We went as far as "China Command" HQ where the General Staff were quartered and had all their peacetime departmental offices, and also the Battle Box, a big concrete dugout 70 feet underground where some of them stayed during the show. . . .

We stayed there another two hours and picked up a few more rations, then moved on down to the centre of the city where they parked us in a small grassy square, and kept us there for another two hours with all the flat-faced fifth columnists of Chinese looking and laughing at us. It was hard to keep from climbing over the fence and kicking their teeth in. We were taken down to the ferry and over to Kowloon, and marched over six miles with our loads until, at about 5:00 p.m., we arrived back in the barracks we had first occupied when we came to China. A more woebegone bunch of Orphan Annies has never been seen. From the 8th of Dec. until the 30th, we had been going most of the time, day and night, being moved from five different camps after we had cleaned them up so they were at least livable. Well, some places had enough food and water, but our trip from the Peak Mansions to the University of Hong Kong with its lack of water was the most trying of all. We were afraid to touch water that hadn't been chlorinated—to get dysentery or cholera at this time would be fatal. We had little or no resistance to combat such awful diseases due to the three weeks we had put in. What a long time three weeks can be.

When we arrived at Nanking Barracks at Shamshuipo it was a shambles. The *dear* Chinese—damn their lousy souls—had absolutely wrecked the place. They had taken every door and window out of the whole place and ripped up every piece of wood they could get their hands on and carted it away. Here we were, in the winter, the weather down to nearly freezing, no stoves, or wood to burn had there been stoves. We spent the first few days cleaning up the place, and believe me, it needed some work. The men had about as much spirit as a soggy cream puff and it was darned hard getting anything done. The first night we slept eight to a room about the size of our living room, on a concrete floor with our clothes on and only one blanket. The windows and doors just holes in the walls to let the wind through. I slept like a top the first night, but until we got some beds rigged up it was a miserable couch to try to rest upon. I managed to scrounge an iron bed and made a mattress of cocoa-nut fibres and dried palm leaves that felt like one of

Eaton's Beauty Sleep springs in comparison with the floor.

On New Year's Eve we dug up a bottle of scotch that had been hoarded for days just for that night, and drank to the health and happiness of our wives and children, hoping they wouldn't be too worried at the lack of news, and hoping that in some mysterious way the thoughts we sent would reach you, and reassure you. I hope they did. On Christmas Eve I thought so much of you two; I pictured Harvelyn's stockings hanging by the fireplace and Santa busy filling them. How I wished I could have been with you, dearest, and seen Punkle get her stockings in the morning. On Jan. 5, Harvelyn's birthday, I lay awake a long time that night, Molly o' mine, thinking of the 11 years that have elapsed since Harvelyn's birth; the awful time you had, how brave you were, how sweet and game you were at all times, and yet within an inch of death all those weeks. There are many things I wish I could do over again, that would make up at least partially for what you have gone through.

One has a lot of time for thought, living as we are. Our life is anything but strenuous. We couldn't stand anything very strenuous in our diet, so we look after our men as best we can, take sun baths, try to find something to read, and every night we are in bed by 8:00 p.m. On New Year's Eve we were regular devils, stayed up until 9:00 p.m. We go to bed because it is easier to keep warm, and there isn't much fun sitting up in the dark, as our candle supply is about gone and we hadn't any fuel to warm us or a place to use it in if we could have found some. Our only fire was at the men's cookhouse, and barely enough to cook the rice properly. Going to bed at such an early hour soon let us catch up on the sleep we lost during December. Of our diet there isn't much to be said in its favour, excepting we are still on our feet. You get rice twice, and occasionally three times a day, providing we save some from our breakfast. Our regular meals were served at 9:00 a.m. and 5:00 p.m. We each had about a pint of boiled rice, mostly just a sticky, glutinous mess with no sugar or milk, unless we were lucky enough to buy some from the Chinese through the fence, at prices 10 times its real worth. Sugar, for instance, sold at eight cents per pound Hong Kong money before the war; we paid one dollar for about three-quarters of a pound and then the ratters put sand in it. Nice people. Our cooks hadn't the proper boilers to cook it properly—*rice*, I mean—so instead of it being dry and flakey, it was a sticky mush. Don't try living on it. You wouldn't relish it very much. Our cooks were really marvellous, though, starting from scratch without one thing to work with; they found some gasoline barrels, cut the tops off them and that was their means of cooking the delectable rice they served. The tinned food we carried with us only lasted a little while. It was used to give a little flavour, and little enough it was at that. I never knew salt had such a delicious taste until we were without it for several weeks. Things taste so damn flat without it, and rice particularly. When we could buy it, we had about two ounces of canned milk and a little sugar with our rice. One tin of milk plus six of water was the mixture we called milk—very rich and strengthening. We sometimes were able to buy buns from the Chinese and really relished them. At home we wouldn't turn one over with a stick if we saw it in the street.

One day we had a banquet, in fact two, while in Shamshuipo. The first one we had rice with bully beef, a few onions and carrots, some peas (tinned ones, of course) and about three potatoes each. They were also tinned ones and about the size of a ping-pong ball. It was a great feed, I can tell you. The other one we had one sausage each, some bully beef, a few peas and three small potatoes. Occasionally we could get a tin of jam and enough that we could have one spoonful each with our rice. We were lucky we had tea twice a day. It was darned weak but hot. It helped a lot; the heat was its only virtue.

I have tried to give a small idea of our actions and mode of life, but from now on it will depend on what the day brings forth. There is much I could write about the lack of co-operation of the Powers That Be, especially one pompous little ass of a brigadier who thinks that such generals as Wellington, Napoleon and other great men were about fit for corporals. There is a conference between a Japanese general and our General Commanding Officer. I hope it will bring forth something that will better conditions for the troops. I am sure that if the Japs were approached in the right manner we could at least have living conditions that would be fit for cattle, and food that would give us a little strength. Rice doesn't seem to stay our hunger for very long, though nobody is really suffering—one can only eat so much then the old system calls a halt.

For the past week we have seen thousands of Chinese refugees going back to where they came from. It was said that over 500,000 flocked into Hong Kong and Kowloon; with them leaving it will mean that many less to feed, and perhaps better conditions. To see them in an endless chain wending their way slowly up through the hills makes one admire their hardiness. They are so slight in build and so thin, and yet they carry incredible loads slung on the end of a bamboo pole. They start sometime before daylight and go in one long stream until afternoon, about 12,000 to 15,000 each day. We can see the road for a distance of about two miles and it is one mass of people. The truck traffic from Hong Kong and Kowloon out into the country is terrific. They must be sacking the two cities completely. There must be a wealth of loot going over the hills.

You remember, Molly, how I had lost my voice while in the Robinson Building. Well, it has stayed with me and has nearly driven me crazy. It is such an effort to make myself heard, and being on the go day and night, and being tired out all the time, didn't improve it any. Everyone could tell where I was by the hoarse croaks I made when speaking. Even the sentries at night recognized me and said, "Pass, Major Baird." Then it got so I couldn't make them hear me, so, as that was inviting a bullet from our own sentries, I had to take a man along to answer the challenges. I hope my voice soon gets better. The last week has rested it considerably and I don't feel the strain quite so much.

We have just had our supper. Our dishes are most elaborate: I have a tomato can as a mess tin and a pineapple tin for a tea cup, a sterling silver spoon and fork, and an ivory-handled knife, the latest models in eating equipment. We had rice, two slices of canned beets, a bit of bread and a little bully beef. These extras are getting scarcer every day. It is getting so scarce, that to get the rice down I would make myself take three spoons of rice then a little bit of beet or bully beef. In this way I made everything come out even and had gotten a little bit of nourishment also. We always saved a little bread until the last. It tasted so good and made us forget the rice for the moment. We were always thinking and dreaming about food. Last night I dreamed Jack Norris and I went back to Wan Chai Gap with a big bunch of trucks to get stores and rations. We loaded them with all kinds of meats, vegetables, fruits, etc., all in tins, of course, and returned back to camp feeling very proud of ourselves. I started to worry about a safe place to put it all where the other units wouldn't raid it. I worried so much that I woke up so darned hungry that it wasn't funny at all. How I wish I could cable you, Dearest. I have not received a letter since leaving home and that seems such a long time ago. I know you will be feeling the same, as I have no idea whether my air mail letter is somewhere at the bottom of the harbour here with Harvelyn's Christmas present of $10 with it. This, of course, we had no control over. Goodnight, Sweetheart. All my love to you both. More later.

[K.}

Friday, January 9, 1942

We got quite excited today over a conference that was to have been held between our General Commanding Officer , Major General Maltby, and a Japanese general. At 2:30 p.m. the Jap general arrived with about 100 soldiers, two machine guns mounted on trucks, and about 15 automobiles. They drew up just outside our quarters. The generals saluted each other a couple of times, the Japs took a number of pictures and then drove away and so all our hopes went flying in a few salutes.

[K.]

A gala day. We had porridge for breakfast, a good dish with a little canned milk. What a change from the everlasting rice. Mostly it is plain boiled rice day in, day out, and it doesn't fatten one at all. The barracks we are in are called Nanking Barracks. The Jubilee Building that had been used as quarters for married officers and NCOs is now used by the officers and NCOs as sleeping quarters and their home in general. Everything that could be removed by the Chinese has been taken. All bathroom taps and most of the fixtures have been either looted or broken. Firewood is so scarce that the inmates are swiping doors from the roof garden to boil the rice with. We have secured our share, too, and promptly reduced them to kindling and thus put them beyond recognition.

They have started to fix up a hospital of sorts. John Crawford said the Japs are sending in 50 beds and I hope some blankets. Many of the men haven't blankets and are sick with dysentery, sleeping on the floor, and at night it is terribly cold. The poor devils are having an awfully thin time of it. The doctors have nothing to treat the men with, and the Japs don't give a damn. So many of the men need dressings and there is practically nothing to do them with. We have so often read of famine and disease running rampant in China and really thought nothing of it as it didn't touch us. Here one gets at least an idea of what it might be. We think in terms of food. We hear of the abundance of foodstuffs at home. Even here there is lots, but the Japs have grabbed it all and, I am sure, are sending it all back to Japan. We were told before the scrap started, the British had food supplies for the English-speaking troops and civilians to last from three to five years and the Japs have garnered that plum also.

Today we are having a little bit of meat with our rice; we have 705 men and we were given about 200 lbs. of meat and bone for all of us. We used to get a 7 lb. roast for ourselves, Molly, so you can see how far this meat issue will go for 705 people. It will flavour our rice, I hope. It is half raining today. Had intended doing the family wash today but it won't dry so will wait "Till the sun shines, Nelly."

[K.]

Sunday, January 11, 1942

The sun is shining in all its glory. I can see thousands of Chinese trekking over the hills. I have been watching them from the balcony of our quarters. The nearest point of the road they are on is about three-quarters of a mile away. Everyone is loaded down with all they can carry. I often watch them through my binoculars and so many are carrying babies. They carry their bundles on bamboo poles

Officer Describes Final Defence Of Hong Kong

Chungking, Jan. 10. (AP)—Oil lamps and candles furnished the light and ponds and wells of brackish water quenched the thirst of Hong Kong's defenders in the last days and nights of the colony under Japanese siege.

The story of the situation before the island stronghold fell to the Japanese on Christmas day was told belatedly today by a British officer, now at Shiunkwan, whose account was circulated by the Chinese News agency.

The water and electrical systems had been knocked out by the Japanese assault. Streets were under constant bombardment from land and air on an ever increasing scale so that distribution of food and supplies had to be undertaken largely during darkness.

Artillery bombardment of key points continued night and day. The Happy Valley and the waterfront area of West Point suffered most heavily. The centre of Victoria, with its more substantial buildings, stood up well, however. The Hong Kong bank, the Gloucester hotel and other landmarks frequently were hit but without significant damage.

A fair proportion of the enemy's shells did not explode.

The central district was at no time blocked by debris and the behavior of the civilian population throughout the siege was excellent, it was said. The civil defence services, managed mainly by Chinese citizens functioned steadily and effectively to the end.

There was no panic or rioting on the island, the British officer said, although organized fifth column activities led to some disorder and looting on the mainland immediately before the Japanese entry.

Article relaying details of the attack on Hong Kong. The Winnipeg Free Press, January 10, 1942.

and shuffle along in a half walk, half run gait that makes their load easier to carry. I wonder where they are all going. This morning we had the last of our porridge for breakfast. I never ate as much of it at one sitting in my life before—a whole tomato can full, with a little milk and sugar on it. It was hot and warmed us through and through. What a wonderful change from rice.

Last night I dreamed of you and Harvelyn, Molly. We were all in the living room. I was sitting by you on the chesterfield, with Harvelyn on my knee but I wakened just as we were called for dinner—darn it! We all seem to think, dream and speak of food, especially just after we get in bed; it is a long time to go from 5:00 p.m. until 9:00 a.m. on a dish of rice, especially when one has to look forward to just another dish of rice. Have had a boil on my cheek during the past week, got some infection when I scratched myself while shaving—every scratch becomes infected in this climate. Had it lanced today, have just had it dressed again.

Oh Sweetheart, I wish I could be with you now and forever. Believe me, any trips I take from now on without you and Harvelyn won't be farther than the corner store. It is 7:15, the sun went down about an hour ago, and it's getting too dark to write. I wish I could eat about a half dozen of the sandwiches we used to make on the Sunday evenings when we were alone. I feel as hollow as a drum, and we had our evening meal only two hours ago—soup. The wind is starting to blow, I feel we are in for a cold night. One blanket and my overcoat just does it for comfort. Good night, Sweetheart.

[K.]

Clear and quite nippy. When I went out to have my morning wash under a tap at the side of the block, my hands nearly froze. The water system in our block has been wrecked, so out we have to go for water. The cold north wind straight from the Gobi Desert seems to find its way through one's clothes and can be darned uncomfortable. Last night more rice came into camp stores, also about 400 pounds of salt for the 5,000 troops that are in this camp. I suppose the Japs will think it should last for about two weeks. After being without salt for over a week, one realizes its value in making food taste better. Our battalion was issued two dozen turnips about the size of my wrist and about six inches long. They will flavour the men's rice slightly—very slightly. . . .

We are jammed in like sardines, but at least we are out of the weather and can keep dry. Being on the third floor should give us some air when the hot weather comes.

Thousands more Chinese are going along the road that disappears over the hill. They are herded like a long line of sheep, all carrying their "all" on their shoulders. Life is very cheap out here. We see bodies floating in the harbour and nobody cares a damn as to the disease they will spread. The other day we were trying to buy some food at the fence, by the waterfront. Where the Chinese gyppers were, lay a dead body. I moved on, having lost interest in food for the time being.

[K.]

Tuesday, January 13, 1942

Last night, when we had all gotten into bed, we were cheering each other up by telling what we would order to eat the first time we have a chance to order a meal. I think we each ordered enough to satisfy the lot of us. Then we got talking about our favourite dishes, especially desserts. It's darn funny what some people like: a custard pudding was one choice. I said one of your pineapple cream puddings or one of Mother's pumpkin pies. One thought of sago pudding. He was greeted with a roar of protest—too much like gooey rice. Our evening meal had been particularly bad. The rice was scorched and they had made a so-called syrup of sugar and water—mostly water—to help it down. It wasn't a recipe that one would get special mention for in the *Good Housekeeping* cookbook. One's mind has to dwell on higher thoughts during such a meal. Today we are having bean soup: just boiled beans with no meat stock or salt. We didn't get any of the salt that came in; our small share went to the men's cookhouse. Still, it will be a change from the eternal rice.

We have been getting some hot rumours the last few days: Germany suing for separate peace with Russia, Japan doing the same with the States.

[K.]

Wednesday, January 14, 1942

When one finishes with the little bit of company work that is to be done, we play a little bridge and read anything we can get our hands on. Have just finished *Old Wine & New*. Not a very cheerful book. There are a lot of Jap ships in the harbour. They are, no doubt, shipping everything that can be moved and that is worth moving, out of the country. Our lunch today was pretty grim: two hardtack biscuits with a very thin smear of sardine between them and two slices of beets

50

and a little weak tea. For supper we have plain rice for a change with a small tea-spoon of jam to make it go down a wee bit easier.

All my smokes are gone. Dad's tin of tobacco was a godsend. I gave about half of it away to the men in my company, a pipeful at a time; I had the last of it this morning. When a person can have a smoke, the lack of food isn't nearly so bad, but from now on I suppose we will all be feeling the need of a cigarette acutely. It will be tough for a while, but most of us are in the same boat.

[K.]

Thursday, January 15, 1942

Ordinarily this would be our mid-month payday, but not today. We couldn't spend it if we had it. Our rations are right down to the bone these days. Just plain rice twice a day and once in a while a few beans. . . . Really they are pretty awful, but we do get enough to keep going on. We are going to have our first cup of black coffee tonight before going to bed. The nights are so long and lonely, sweetheart. I can't sleep more than seven hours so I lay awake for hours in the early morning wishing I could see you and Harvelyn. I haven't said very much, dear, but how I miss you and Punkle. Goodnight, dearest—oh! a naval chap has just dropped in and is giving some cheerful news. I hope it may be true.

[K.]

Friday, January 16, 1942

Another hot rumour. We have heard the Japs are ready to move on an hour's notice. Hope it is true. . . . We had our first decently cooked rice this morning. It was quite dry, flakey, but then I was darned hungry too.

[K.]

Saturday, January 17, 1942

Just 41 days ago this morning, at 8:00 a.m., the scrap started, and how long ago it seems. During the first 18 days we were going day and night with little time off for sleep, and meals that were most irregular. But there always was plenty to eat had we wanted it or had time to go for it. Since the 25th of Dec. we have been like tramps, eating out of tin cans or anything we could get to hold our food in. Now it is rice, rice, rice. We live on what the Japs allow us—*rice*. They give us a little meat once in a while, but there is so little of it we send it to the men's kitchen. It just about gives a little flavour to the rice. We live on exactly what the men do, supplemented occasionally by the little we can buy through the fence. No matter what we try to do for the men, there are a number of trouble makers that one feels like borrowing one of the sentry's rifles and going to town. We have some of the yellowest scum that any unit could be cursed with, but then one can hardly wonder. We needed 200 extra men when we were ordered to move. The various training centres sent us their sweepings. There were of course some darn good men among them—some of the best—but about three-quarters of them were worthless and not worth the powder to blow them to hell. And then add to that about 10 per cent of our own men, and you have enough to play the devil with what otherwise is a darn good battalion. Our new officers all are keen chaps and we like them, but if we could get hold of the people responsible for sending that lot of trash they would wish they hadn't been born. The wind is cold and goes right through one. Our only interest is getting rumours, probably all lies, but we all look forward to them. We aren't suffering one little bit but are all terribly fed up on our rations and the lack of smokes.

[K.]

Hong Kong Force Fought Till Exhausted

Chungking, Jan. 19. (AP)—Britain's gallant garrison at Hong Kong fought until it was blind and feeble from exhaustion, an official who escaped just before the crown colony fell to the Japanese said yesterday.

David MacDougall, representative of the ministry of information, said the Japanese navy kept a respectful distance during the siege, which ended in surrender Christmas Day.

Only once a light cruiser was sighted," he said. "We opened up on her at once and scored at least one hit. She quickly retired."

Paying tribute to the greatly outnumbered defenders, which included Canadians, MacDougall said:

"I saw 17 men returning from the front line and they were barely able to stand. They were led up to the shelters like blind men, they were so exhausted."

MacDougall was wounded in the left shoulder during his escape.

The Winnipeg Free Press, *January 19, 1942.*

Sunday, January 18, 1942

At 8:00 a.m. I watched two sticks of bombs leave two planes and sail in our direction. Everyone felt they would land in their laps. The nearest was about 200 feet away and when we got our Adams apples where they are supposed to be on duty, we knew for sure things had started. How I wish I knew how you both are, and most of all I wish you could know that I am all right and longing to see you both. There is so little to write about and I am sure things will be repeated over and over again as I recall things, forgetting I may already have mentioned them. There have been all kinds of weird and wonderful rumours lately. This morning one of the navy officers came in and said they were all wrong, so we feel let down, yet we all felt they were just a bunch of nice thoughts somebody started on the rounds. Confirmed rumours are very few and far between. We have just finished our Sunday night supper, some fried rice with a little dab of marmalade on it. The latter tasted great. It had some taste to it. Good night, Sweetheart.

[K.]

Wednesday, January 21, 1942

Haven't had anything to write about for the past few days. We have had about 40 men returned to us during the last two days—also Major Hodkinson; Capt. Terry, our paymaster; Capt. Prendergast; Capt. Laite, our padre; and Capt. Porteous, our auxiliary services officer. We now have two suites in the Jubilee Bldg. Our accommodation for cooking is becoming very strained, we have reached our limit. Trading over the fence is becoming a thing of the past and when it ceases it will be pretty awful just living on rice without a little sugar and much watered milk on it. The Japs are shooting the Chinese that bring things to the fence for sale. Last Sunday they shot two girls, just youngsters about 12 years old, killing them both. Life is very much in the raw here and life is held very cheaply.

There have been quite a few deaths from dysentery here, mostly among the Indian troops, and when the hot weather comes they tell us it will be a regular death trap. Cheerful, aren't they! The weather lately has been lovely, the days nice and bright but fairly chilly in the wind. There are always rumours that either buck us up or let us down. So life goes on. We are told the Indian troops are going out. I hope they leave, they are a dirty looking lot of cut-throats. I hope they bring the other Canadian battalion here, or send us to North Point camp where the Royal Rifles of Canada now are. If they bring them here, we will be in sufficient numbers to make ourselves heard. We have been discriminated against in every way. I thought I was in for a cold last night; am still sore all over, but hope I have it broken.

[K.]

Friday, January 23, 1942

Have had a rotten cold the last three days and have felt like hell. The rations have been pretty awful. I have had a temperature of about 101. One just can't stay in bed, it is too hard to lie on with comfort. It is a pleasure to get up in the morning; when one has to go to bed between 8:00 p.m. and 9:00 p.m., morning seems a long way off.

Last night we were making arrangements to move from where we have been quite comfortable to another part of the barracks that the Indians had just vacated. The huts are absolutely filthy. The CO troops insisted on our moving: just another one of the British officers' ideas of playing the game. As a body they are the most selfish bunch of prigs I have ever met. We had to go so that some artillery officers that are arriving could have our quarters. We were all up in arms and going to raise hell about it when about 6:00 p.m. the Col. was called over to the general's quarters to see a Japanese officer. He was told we were to go back to Hong Kong to North Point camp. We were tickled pink to be rid of the Imperial troops, damn them. We got up early and moved off about 10:00 a.m. I felt like the devil, still had a bit of temperature and was as weak as a kitten. Before we had gone half a mile I was wishing they would halt for a rest. We were loaded down with everything we owned and it was awkwardly packed. A kit bag, a haversack and a roll of blankets aren't the easiest things to carry even if they aren't so awfully heavy, but they kept right on going and never halted until we reached the ferry—about four miles of it, and the last half mile seemed longer than all the rest. I had about 75 lbs. to carry and it weighed 200 before we arrived. Everyone was the same. There were a good many white faces when we finally found a seat on the ferry. It had been some walk without a rest, but they made up for it by bringing us within one-quarter of a mile of our destination.

When we finally got settled in the camp, the Rifle officers gave us some tea and buns and canned fruit. It tasted heavenly. For supper that night we had a real meat stew with vegetables of all kinds in it, as much as we could eat, tea with milk and sugar, and canned peaches. All the time they have been here they have been living like that and don't know what rice tastes like. They were allowed to go out and bring in supplies and they brought in plenty. We also had biscuits with plenty of butter on them. I wish the bunch at our other barracks could have seen us tuck it in and still not be able to participate. A nice thought. Eh! Well! We all feel very strongly against them though I suppose we will soon forget all the small and mean things they did to us.

The Japs have said there are only two sets of troops in the field: the Indians, because they encountered them first, and the Canadians. This move has made me feel we are getting somewhere. I hope our casualty list has reached home by now. It is getting too dark to write. Goodnight, Sweetheart.

[K.]

Saturday, January 24, 1942

This morning we had porridge, jam, biscuits, butter, and tea with milk and sugar. What a change from what we have been having. Am still feeling as though

The Argyle Street Officers' Camp
The above huts were erected by the Hong Kong Government as temporary quarters for the Chinese soldiers who, having crossed the British border during the Sino-Japanese war in 1939, were interned by the British Authorities. For a year and a half these huts were used as an Officers POW Camp. Triple barbed wire, electric circuit fences and flood-lamps were erected by the Japanese to prevent escape.

I have just passed through a knot-hole backwards. The trip plus my cold has pulled me down a bit. Capt. Robt. Philip came in today from Argyle. Came with a number of our men and NCOs. We are gradually getting them all back. Tonight we had another banquet: a big dish of pea soup, half a tin of bully beef, cheese, bread with jam on it, and tea with milk and sugar. What a meal. The men had the same and everyone has taken a new lease on life. It can't last, of course, but while it does we can take it. It did my heart good to hear the Ahs! and Ahs! of the boys when their meal was being served—everyone needed the extra rations so badly. I have lost 36 pounds in weight and find the least bit of exertion is hard work. Harvelyn, you wouldn't have a chance to tease me about my tummy now. It just doesn't show at all. Am quite proud of my girlish figure though it seems to be covered with knobs and bumps in places.

[K.]

Sunday, January 25, 1942

Three months ago today we pulled out of Winnipeg. And what a mistake was made in sending us here. It is just one month today since the truce was declared.

At this hour one month ago we were being plastered with everything the Japs had on their menu: machine guns, trench mortars, both large and small artillery up to six-inch shells. Then we had nine planes that seemed to be doing nothing but trying to wipe the four houses my company occupied ... and succeeded admirably as we were driven from the forward houses and retired to the ones a little way back. They caught us in the open. We felt like so many peanuts on an elephant's back—no cover and all hoping their aim would be poor. Fortunately it was. Then when we made a dash for cover, they laid down a fire so intense we daren't stick our noses out. We had several wounded, some in quite bad shape. They begged not to be left behind—we hadn't any intention of ever leaving them behind. They all reached hospital and were taken care of. Those that could walk did; the rest were carried.

This morning we had a church parade on the square. The Royal Rifles of Canada, the [Royal] Navy and naval forces, some Dutch prisoners from a sub that arrived in camp yesterday and the Grenadiers, about 2,500 in all. We all live in an area much smaller than the school block between Fifth and Sixth streets in Brandon. Our huts are very much like the sheep pens at the Brandon Fair Grounds, only all enclosed. When the British troops moved out they left the place in the most filthy condition. They are a bunch of hot citizens, and the part that hurts is that their officers above the rank of Capt. are the most snooty and inhuman lot I have ever met. We would have had much better treatment from the Japs if it weren't for those pig-headed asses. I never thought I would put on paper my thoughts about senior British officers, but I can now understand why we are so damn backward in this war. I could be court-martialled for what I think.

[K.]

Monday, January 26, 1942

Had pancakes for breakfast. They weren't exactly prize-winners, but tasted like a million with a little corn syrup on them, three per officer. Could have stood about 10 more, but even if one leaves the table hungry at times, the variety we are getting helps a lot. Being without smokes is not a pleasant thing to go through. We are all about crazy at times for a drag at the old fag, especially in the middle of the night when one wakens and can't go back to sleep again.

[K.]

Thursday, January 29, 1942

Hello, Sweetheart,

There has been nothing to write about the past three days, except that a number of the navy escaped and the Japs are darned angry about it and have said that if any more try to escape and get away they will take reprisals. They have been fairly decent with us, though. And we are living ever so much better than we were. We have been getting meat every day and some greens. We get bread once in a while with a little jam or corn syrup, about a spoonful at a time (I am afraid it can't last for very much longer), some milk in our tea and at night some cocoa. This doesn't happen every day, but two or three times a week. The amount of solid food, excepting rice, is extremely small and as most of our diet is more or less liquid, we all spend most of our nights going to visit the little house around the corner. It plays hell with one's rest, though one would think we had nothing to do but rest. Our food doesn't seem to give us any real strength at all. We are more or less feeling washed out all the time.

I made a cribbage board yesterday with practically no tools, and believe me it looks it too, but we can play cribbage on it and that is what I made it for. Am starting on a pair of wooden sandals as I have only one pair of shoes and they may have to do me for many months to come. I worry a lot about you two,

Sweetheart, because I know you haven't any news of us at all and no chance of getting any for months to come. I wish I could get a thought wave through to you and let you know we are all right. It would give us both a little peace of mind. There are about 688 of our grenadiers in this camp, with about 75 more in hospital. So our losses were about 150 killed, all in about one week's time. Good night, Sweetheart.

Best love to you both,
Ken

Saturday, January 31, 1942

It seems such a long time since New Year's Eve—just one month. We went to Shamshuipo on Dec. 30 and one month has seemed to stretch into an eternity. Yesterday we had a Jap general visit us. He will be in charge of the Hong Kong district and we hope he will contact Canada with our casualty list.

[K.]

Huts—Shamshuipo Camp
Life in a POW Camp controlled by the Japanese was reduced to an almost primitive exis-
tence. Fundoshi, traditional Japanese loincloths, became the most popular garment and a
craving for food the most exciting emotion.

Kitchen—Shamshuipo Camp
For forty-four months, men were forced to live on a rice diet approximately equal to half of what a coolie would normally eat. Pellagra and beriberi, with their attendant physical degeneration, swept through the Camp. Of all the Red Cross food parcels sent to Hong Kong not one prisoner received more than seven in 44 months of captivity.

Have just finished breakfast, which consisted of a half tomato can of porridge and about one-sixth of a cup of condensed milk and water, two teaspoons of corn syrup and a half slice of bread. The bread was made in our own ovens by the cook staff—a *Dutch oven* and works awfully well too. We also had a little tea. It all tasted like a banquet. We could have enjoyed twice as much but had enough to keep going on.

The fog and clouds are very low this morning, they come sailing over the hills from the sea, it feels like rain. We have heard so much about the rainy season that we all dread it, as we are in such cramped quarters. There are about 75 in our hut. It is 20 feet wide by 120 feet long and when you have beds and all our belongings in that space—well! There just isn't much room to cavort around in.

The flies are simply awful; it is a fight every noon and evening to see who gets the food. We kill thousands each day, but the supply seems inexhaustible. Have just finished lunch, plain rice with one little sardine to flavour it, no milk or sugar, and some clear tea. There is a ball game on now between our officers and the officers of the Royal Rifles of Canada. . . . Have just bought a cake of soap. Guess we will have to go dirty when all our money is gone.

[K.]

There has been so little to write about but each day I think so much of you, Dear, and hope you are not worrying too much. Yesterday the Japs held a muster parade to see that none had escaped. We were found OK. Dysentery is on the increase and this will be a very unhealthy spot, I am afraid, when the hot weather comes. The number of flies is beyond belief: we are doing everything possible to combat them. A lot of the men are mere shadows of what they used to be. We all have lost pounds. I am quite willowy, having lost 36 pounds since leaving home, no paunch at all. I wish I could see you two today, Sweetheart. I can't see any ray of hope for an early release, especially the way the war seems to be going.

[K.]

Thursday, February 12, 1942

Hello, Sweethearts,

Every day and night I keep thinking of you and wondering how you both are. The hard part is not knowing whether you have had any news from the Japs about us. I don't suppose you have. We have supplied the Japs with all the necessary information several times but don't suppose anything has been done by the little devils and I know how everyone must be worrying and wondering. It seems years since we left and as yet not one bit of mail has arrived for anyone. I have often wondered just what stand the government is taking and what they say and what the Opposition in the House at Ottawa is saying; it will be very interesting to look up the back copies of the press and read about ourselves and then see how much was *really* known about it all in Canada.

The situation here is about the same. They have cut our rations down again. Believe me, when one gets up from a meal still feeling as though the meal hadn't been served as yet, the next meal seems a long way off. Our rice has been cut in half and to replace it we get two slices of bread per day—without butter, of course. Yesterday we had for breakfast plain rice and one cup of tea; it was awful. For lunch we had 3 oz. of bully beef, two slices of bread, and tea. You can see, Sweetheart, there is so little to write about that I have been writing about our food. I must stop this nonsense as we are getting to do nothing but think, talk and dream of food, especially when one goes for 15 hours from supper to breakfast. All our favourite dishes parade themselves, most attractively I must admit, through our dreams. We never thought the old tummy could be such an important bit of ourselves. It has been very cold and raw. Everyone feels the dampness so much we sleep with our clothes on sometimes, but then one feels so darned grubby in the morning. Most of us have only one blanket, so we stay dressed.

[K.]

Saturday, February 14, 1942

How I wish I could be your Valentine today, Sweethearts. It would be so wonderful to just ring the door bell and stay home for always. They can have as many

Proper Feeding Promised by Japs

London, Feb. 13. (CP)—In connection with fears expressed in some quarters as to how European prisoners might fare on the Japanese rice diet, the Japanese government has announced that it will "take account of national and racial customs on the basis of reciprocity" in feeding and clothing its prisoners.

The war office, reporting this last night, said also that Japan had agreed to observe the Geneva convention, with whatever alterations might be necessary regarding British Empire prisoners of war.

The Winnipeg Free Press,
February 13, 1942.

wars from now on as they like; I will say good luck but I won't be in it. We have been having perfectly devilish weather here lately. The cold is the kind that goes right through one. None of us have been warm or comfortable for at least two weeks and the food is pretty awful.

[K.]

Thursday, February 19, 1942

Haven't written anything for several days. No news or anything of interest and so the silence. The food has been better the last few days—better prepared and a little sugar and milk with the rice. It doesn't take much to make us think we have had a banquet!

Tomorrow the new Japanese governor is arriving. There will be a lot of rejoicing among the Japs. They do everything by numbers: smile, scowl, etc., etc. No individuality at all. Now that Singapore has fallen, I wonder what is in store for us. Oh, Dearest! If I only knew that you and Harvelyn are all right and for you to know that I am all right, I would have a lot more peace of mind. The loss of Singapore came as a great jolt to us. We thought our defenses were really good but it just goes to show how damnably unprepared we were.

Our men are building new cookers in the kitchens. It really is wonderful what they have done, and the results we are getting are wonderful. When they can get the flour to cook with (from what we hear we are going to have some pretty slim meals as summer comes and passes. I hope the rumours are wrong) the bakers turn out fine biscuits and really wonderful bread. But when one has only rice to go with it, it gets pretty awful, although it is much better than Shamshuipo.

It is awful to look out in the harbour and see about 30 of our cargo boats that have all been scuttled by our sailors so that the Japs wouldn't get at them. Millions of dollars' worth of ships and cargo resting on the bottom of the harbour. The Japs are sending down divers and unloading the ships and will no doubt float the boats again and have a lot more ships to use against us, the b——. It is hell to be without smokes, especially when the food is so limited; one feels hungry all the time. Have a rash all over me that nearly drives me insane, a sort of dermatitis. That plus a rotten cold makes life very cheery. The M.O. [medical officer] says it is caused by a lack of vitamin B in our diet and to expect all kinds of funny things to develop among the troops. Bye for now.

Love,
Ken

Saturday, February 21, 1942

In three months' time you will have another birthday. Sweetheart, how I wish I could be with you by that time. I never thought I would be 10,000 miles away from you—ever in my life—and believe me I hate every one of the 10,000 miles. It will take so long to return once we start. I wonder when that will be. We have just had another inoculation, this time for cholera. I got quite a shock when John Crawford stuck the needle in me; it didn't hurt, but I just then realized how thin my arms were. They are about the size of yours, but lack the beauty yours have. Mine are angles and knobs instead of curves like yours. The weather continues to be cold and raw, with a wind that whistles through our huts and seems to find us out without any trouble. The nights are the worst. How I wish I could cuddle up beside you and get warm. The new governor has taken over. I hope the rations improve; if they don't it will be darn serious for our camp from a health point of view.

[K.]

Saturday, February 28, 1942

Haven't written anything for several days, there has been nothing to write about. Yesterday we opened up our own kitchen for the Officers' Mess and had

Estimate 296 Dead, Missing At Hong Kong

Ottawa, Feb. 26. (CP)—News that 296 Canadian soldiers are dead or missing after the losing battle fought by Canadian and empire troops against the Japanese at Hong Kong, was given the house of commons yesterday.

The information came from Defence Minister Ralston in a brief statement. He had no further information about the 1,985 Canadian officers and men who went to Hong Kong in mid-November.

Actually, Col. Ralston's information, relayed to Canada from Japan by way of Argentina, said only that Canadian prisoners of war taken at Hong Kong numbered 1,689.

But from that figure Col. Ralston deduced that 296 "would be regarded as either dead or missing." Said Col. Ralston.

"The message is extremely vague. It gives figures and that is all.

"The statement is that Japanese government officially indicate figures for prisoners of war, Hong Kong, Canadians, 1,689.

"Honorable members will remember that the number who embarked was 1,985. So that means, on the basis of those figures, I sincerely regret to say, at least without further information, that 296 would be regarded as either dead or missing."

First Information

The defence minister said that this was the first official information from which any definite conclusion could be arrived at with respect to the number of Canadian casualties at Hong Kong.

Until yesterday there had been virtually no news of the fate of Canadians who fought at Hong Kong with other British and Empire troops until compelled to surrender Christmas Day.

Among those known to be killed were Brig. J. K. Lawson, the commanding officer, of Ottawa, and his chief of staff, Col. P. Hennessey, of Ottawa.

A royal commission inquiry into the sending of Canadians to Hong Kong is scheduled to start its hearing next week with Sir Lyman P. Duff as a royal commissioner.

The Winnipeg Free Press,
February 26, 1942.

74

the best meal in over two months—rice and a stew made of vegetables, and a little meat gravy. Our breakfasts have been the best meal of the day: a little sweetened rice and a bit of milk and some cocoa. Lunch, very slim, mostly just bread and tea. The Japs have cut our original rice ration in half. I think they must be trying to wean us from eating altogether. We get a little fresh meat once in a while, about 100 lbs. for 700 men. It cooks up into a sort of gravy that helps to flavour the rice a little. We have had whale steaks and I like them—they taste fishy, but give us something to chew on. The meat looks like beef. They have given us octopus or squid; it is pretty awful, very much like a boiled inner tube of an auto tire. It all tasted good as it was different and we like the change.

The cold is still with us and more rain. I am wondering what it will be like in these cramped quarters when the heat and rainy season set in. We aren't looking forward to it at all. I wish I knew how you and Punkle are today. I would feel so much better to know that you were all right. We never get any news of Canada at all. I wish England would send a message about Canada to us. We sometimes get a little news and wonder just how authentic it is. I have found a piece of sheet brass* that has been through a fire. I am going to try and make something out of it. It will be an awful job smoothing out the surface and polishing it, but I have

* This was part of a shell casing.—*Ed*.

plenty of time on my hands and it will give me something to do. I haven't any kind of tools but will get Cpl. Oomen to make what I need. He is really very clever at making things of that kind. Good night, Sweetheart.

Best love,
Ken

Tuesday, March 3, 1942

Still cold and raw. Our rations for lunch today consisted of eggs of very obscure and doubtful origin. Age positively unknown but suspected of being about one year or more old. Hungry as I was, I took my bread and tea and called it a meal, and the hell of it is there are more for tomorrow. I wish they would give us something worth eating.

[K.]

Saturday, March 7, 1942

Cold and raining. It is just 10:00 a.m. I have been reading for a while, as has everyone else. Lt. Corrigan is playing "In the Mood" on a saxophone. Yesterday it was nice and warm but everyone is shivering today. The lack of news is our greatest worry. News from home would cheer us up no end and put us all on our feet again. If there were only some way of communicating with you and getting a letter once in a while from you, it would be just plain heaven. I miss you and Harvelyn so much, dearest.

Our hut is awfully crowded. It is about 120 by 18 or 20 feet, and about 75 live in it so our space is darned limited. Some of the beds are double deckers at that, so we seem to be living in a second-hand junk shop, everything is hung on lines or from the rafters. We are living on the edge of the city of Victoria with a population of nearly one million, yet being a prisoner of war leaves us feeling as though we are alone on another planet. I ate two and a half eggs yesterday, and though it took a lot of will power to get them down, I feel a lot better having had some solid food for a change. Rice is all right but lordy, how one gets fed up on it after eating it every day for months and most days little else. Have just finished lunch, three pancakes and a little sugar syrup. Aunt Jemima never made pancakes that tasted as good as these did. They were really delicious. I could have eaten another four or five. Since we have had our own kitchen and cook, our meals have improved and taste more like food should. Tonight we have cuttlefish in some form or other, and if you have never revelled in the joys of a dish of boiled inner tubes

Interior of Huts—Shamshuipo Camp
Bed-bugs were everywhere: in beds, stools, chairs, clothing, headgear, etc. One couldn't sit peacefully on a stool or sleep quietly in one's bed. Hot water and insect powder were not allowed for de-bugging. Some experimented with bedbug traps, with dubbin and lime, but without success. The best remedy was to acquire immunity.

78

then you have yet one more experience to thrill your palate. They are awful! I have just remembered that last Tuesday was Dad's birthday. I wish I could have said greetings to him. If I could have done that, I would be with you, Dearest. That is all that will ever matter for me for the rest of my life.

[K.]

Wednesday, March 11, 1942

Last night we had a good meal, our tummies were comfortably filled. We had some boiled pork, rice, turnips and gravy. It tasted awfully good as our rations have been on the slim side lately. No bread for a week, only rice and turnips, and believe me it isn't a diet to get fat on or to go into convulsions of rapture over. More squid. They are like small octopus. The Japs have taken every flashlight and camera and tools of every kind. Our repair men are in an awful fix for things to work with and the huts need so much work to make them rainproof. We are supposed to have a visit from Col. Tokunaga, who is in charge of all prison camps.

Ken

We have just been told that we will soon be able to send some form of communication home to our families. Oh, Sweetheart! It would be so wonderful to have some word of you two, and to be able to let you know that I am all right. It would give me a lot of peace of mind to know that you are both well. . . .

The Jap commander has told us we will receive some pay each month. It will allow us to buy something to help this awful diet and to buy a smoke once in a while. Our meals will be awful for a while, then improve for a day or two, then go back to where they were—*just plain bad* and never enough to really fill one up. Breakfast always seems so small after 16 hours since last night's supper. We always are hungry. Not the starving feeling, but just darn uncomfortable. One could write out the meals we are to get a week in advance and not be very far out in one's guess.

There have been a number of corpses floating around in the tide in front of our lines. They are not pretty at all; the tide has taken them away now, thank the Lord. If such a thing happened at home, all the police in the country would be trying to find out all about it. The Japs weren't a bit interested. We miss getting the news so much; the papers here only publish what the Japs want the public to know and never anything showing they have had a loss. We are inclined to be a bit crabby, but sufficient food and smokes plus some work would soon put us on our feet. Three years ago now we were in Brandon on our leave and all three of us sick. Not much fun was had. I hope you both have been well this past winter.

[K.]

Wednesday, March 25, 1942

Haven't written for several days—nothing to write about. Have just finished lunch: one slice of bread, a little jam and tea. I was hungry before lunch but now feel really ravenous. We just had enough to tease us. What I could do to one of your roast beef dinners, Sweetheart, right this minute! Last night was one of our lucky days for a meal. We had fried rice done in peanut oil, boiled rice, a little piece of pork, a slice of bread and tea. But days like this are very rare. We have had eggs several times. It would be interesting to know the date they were laid, but I am sure it is best that we don't. I hope the pay comes along soon, we haven't any soap and that is really a necessity in a place like this. Also, a mosquito net. The devils chew us to pieces at night. The season for malaria is on us. We will be lucky if we escape it as they say the mosquitos here are the malarial kind. Everyone is dreading the hot weather with the possibilities of cholera and dysentery.

The rats have been pretty bad but are being brought under control; they bring the cholera and it is deadly. We don't get any news but what we read in the Jap papers and it is so one-sided and discouraging.

[K.]

Friday, March 27, 1942

Good Friday. Attended church service on the parade ground, along with about 300 others. I thought of you and Harvelyn and offered up a prayer for your health and happiness. I wondered what you were doing at that hour. Our padre preached the sermon. He is a good speaker and a darn nice chap. We received an awful shock in the afternoon: the Japs came in and paid us. We all promptly bought cigarettes at exorbitant prices. We hadn't had any for two and a half months. [With] the excitement of having some money and smoking ten times too much, I never closed my eyes all night. We are being paid 110 yen per month. Military yen. They aren't worth a damn, excepting in occupied territories. The regular Jap yen sold for 7.5 for $1.00 before the war started, so you can see how wealthy we are. They are charging the Canadian govt. 60 yen per month for the food they bring us (for each of us). I got three small tins of condensed milk and had half of one with my rice this morning. It was darn good, I can tell you. The tins are about the size of the little tins of vegetables we used to get for Harvelyn when she was a baby. They cost two for one yen. I am trying to buy some sheets and pyjamas and towels and a pillow slip. At present my sleeping equipment consists of one blanket on a wooden bed with three rice sacks stretched across as a mattress. Have just been down in the Rifles' end of the hut watching the ants go after the bed bugs. They make a good job of it too. My bed is anything but a Beauty Rest mattress. I have become quite used to the bumps and jumps, but one thin blanket doesn't keep out the damp cold that creeps around us at night. Lots of the men haven't even one blanket and some nights have been terribly cold. I have two sets of undies, two pr. Khaki shorts, three shirts, one hat that is too small, one pr. shoes, three pr. socks. The well-dressed officer, I can tell you.

[K.]

Sunday, April 5, 1942

Easter Sunday morning. Greetings, Sweethearts. Have just come from church parade all dressed in my fine wardrobe. It was quite in keeping with everyone else. I prayed for three things for you and Harvelyn, Molly Dearest: good health, peace of mind and happiness, because if you have these three things I too will be happy. I sincerely hope you have them, Dearest.

Last night I had a good sleep, was really tired having stayed awake all the night before. The days are getting hotter; fortunately, they are partly cloudy. We are all dreading the summer from May until October. They tell us it is pretty awful, the humidity is very trying. However, we will deal with it when it arrives, and won't let a little thing like that get us down. We greet each morning with a smile, knowing it is one day nearer home and loved ones. It will be so wonderful when that day arrives. I wakened at 6:00 this morning and indulged in the joy of a cigarette. We have been so long without them, the past two days we all have smoked too many. As I lay there I thought of you and Harvelyn going to church and of Harvelyn being up early hunting Easter eggs. I felt so lonely, Sweetheart. I know the long and lonely evenings you have spent, so have I, but we have at least had peace of mind in one way and are free from one of our worries. That has helped me a lot to carry on at times when things looked sort of dark and blue.* Just outside my window some of the navy chaps are playing mah jong, all stripped to the waist getting tanned. Some of them are as brown as old leather. We receive 110

* Here my father is referring to the fact that he and the other soldiers knew that their families were safe in Canada.—*Ed*.

84

yen per month and pay so much into the mess to buy sugar, canned milk, bully beef and whatever else we can to make the rice more palatable. Meat is nearly unheard of. We have to pay such prices for everything. The canteen brings in 12 oz. of butter ($9.30 Chinese money) and it would make very indifferent cooking butter at that. For an 8 oz. bottle of honey, $2.50; a bar of chocolate that costs 5 cents at home, $1.30 here, nearly 20 cents in our money. And it seems like looted stock at that, or seized goods, so they are making a huge profit. Well, sweetheart, it is somewhere around 10:00 p.m. at home. I have been wondering if you and Harvelyn went to Brandon. If so, you will likely be having sandwiches, coffee and cake. How I wish I were with you. Night, dear.

[K.]

Easter Monday, April 6, 1942
I hope it is a better day at home than here, it has been raining since 5:00 p.m. yesterday. We have had three RED LETTER DAYS. Friday, payday, too many smokes and no sleep. Sunday, Harry Hook produced a 26 oz. crock and we had a good slug. It had a kick like a mule, having been without a drink for over three months—we enjoyed it. This morning we had oatmeal with a half cup of milk and

toast with some butter on it. The toast, the first we have had, was delicious. How the cooks produced it I don't know. After the meals we have been having since becoming prisoners, breakfast was a banquet. Turned quite cold during the night and we all felt kind of chilly. Have secured a pair of pyjamas and a towel, and am on the lookout for some sheets and pillow slips. We are living as they used to 1,000 years ago, bartering. We can't use money excepting to buy cigarettes, so they are the medium of exchange. The navy have things to sell. Our money comes in 10 yen notes so we can't make change, so cigarettes are used. I bought a sun helmet for 30 cigarettes and have made an offer of 30 cigs. for two sheets.

[K.]

Friday, April 10, 1942

On Tuesday morning the Japs came in and said Col. Sutcliffe had died on Monday evening at 6:00 p.m. He had been taken to hospital on Wednesday. He had been suffering from dysentery, anemia, malnutrition and a touch of malaria. It all pulled him down so he just hadn't the strength to stand it. No one has very much reserve vitality to draw upon. The food we receive doesn't build strength and for two months we were hungry all the time. It is just a darn shame that he

86

was taken. He did his darnedest during the scrap, under conditions that were practically impossible—lack of co-operation and no information from the Battle Box—what I think of their darned incompetence. Lew never spared himself and consequently was in a very run-down condition. I am so sorry for Mrs. Sutcliffe. Major Trist is now CO and Harry Hook, 2IC [second in command]. Since the Col.'s death the Japs are getting our people to the hospital in a hurry now, instead of taking a couple of days to do it.

It has made an awful difference to our mess since being paid, a little extra to eat, and some smokes, everything is so expensive. The NCOs and men haven't been paid, so we hand out a lot of smokes, and it keeps us broke all the time. However, we are darned glad to do all we can. I know what it is to be out of smokes—so I am an easy mark—but not too easy.

[K.]

Tuesday, April 14, 1942

Haven't written anything for the past few days. Have been nursing a boil on my nose, putting hot compresses on every two hours. A boil doesn't seem to inspire me to write glowing accounts of what is happening. As a matter of fact,

Col. J.L.H. Sutcliffe

Commanding Officer George Trist

nothing does happen. All this I have written may never be seen by anyone, but it helps fill in the time. The days are getting hot and the mosquitos are in swarms, so I suppose malaria will be the next thing to contend with. We changed our beds around yesterday. They are better spaced, we have a little more room and air. What it will be like when the summer arrives, we hate to think. The parade ground is about the size of the playground between the two schools on Fifth St., and for 2,000 troops to exercise on that area, it seems more like a crowded ball room floor. There are no trees, just the huts for shade. It is now about 7:45 p.m. in Winnipeg. Punkle will be out playing. I am sure the skipping rope or roller skates will be worked fairly strenuously these days or maybe she has her bike. I hope she has one, but am afraid of them where the traffic is so heavy.

[K.]

Saturday, April 16, 1942

Five months ago today we landed in this blasted country. It seems twice that length of time, so many things have happened. It is really hot today; we haven't anything to do but try to keep cool. We have two parades a day, morning and evening, just to call the roll and P.T. [Physical Training] after morning parade for about 20 minutes. Clothes and shoes are a serious problem as the mosquito season is just starting. Bought a pair of white slacks for 30 cigs. They will keep the little pests off my legs. . . . The Japs are starting to build a new wire entanglement around our camp and are electrifying it. They have brought in truckloads of wire. We had an awful time trying to get barbed wire during the war, now the Japs have unlimited supplies. The boil on my nose broke yesterday. I feel and look more like a human being. I think of you two all the time. If only we could get mail to each other, it would help so much. Unless they send in rations today, we will have just plain rice. We haven't fared badly since coming here, but Shamshuipo is still a ghastly nightmare.

[K.]

Sunday, April 19, 1942

Yesterday, two officers and 20-odd men came back to us. All the navy moved out of this camp; they seem to be concentrating all the Canadians in one camp. I felt sorry for the naval men moving, it simply poured. Everyone was soaked and cold. They had to stand on the parade square for hours in the rain; all their kits were opened and got soaking wet. There will no doubt be a lot of sickness among them as there were a lot of them over 60 years of age and had come off the retired list when the war started. Our quarters are being re-allotted and everyone is busy cleaning huts. They were left in a filthy mess. We are hoping for better food supplies too.

[K.]

Thursday, April 23, 1942

Last night I dreamed of you and Harvelyn and was so let down when I wakened up and found myself still in China. How far away you are, Dearest. I hope you both are all right. . . . Vic Dennis is in hospital. A large piece of wood fell on his foot and he has gone up for an X-ray. He was in a lot of pain for a few days. We play softball and volleyball for exercise, but it doesn't take much to tire us out on the scanty rations we receive. It would take months to get us in shape for action, living on the best of rations.

[K.]

Saturday, April 25, 1942

Six months ago today we left home. What a mistake. Four months ago at this time we were being shelled and bombed unmercifully. They literally blasted us out of the houses we were occupying and then shelled us along the roads as we were going to the Peak. When we arrived at the Peak we found an armistice had been signed. Everyone was in a jumpy state; the reaction from the tension being so sudden left everyone pretty jittery. There were few dry eyes among us as we thought we only had about 300 all ranks left in our battalion. After 18 days and nights of practically no sleep, we all felt pretty low in our minds. We ran into so many unpleasant and maddening experiences at the hands of our higher commands, they will always remain in our memories as the biggest piece of pig-headedness and inefficiency that could possibly happen. It continued right through Shamshuipo prison camp, also from the naval higher-ups in Shamshuipo. They have tried it here at North Point, but soon found out it didn't work. It is great here now, comparatively speaking, we have twice as much room and can have at least breathing room. This morning it simply poured with rain. In about one month's time the rainy season starts. In less than a month you will have your birthday, Sweetheart. How I wish I could be with you. I hope mail will start arriving soon, both from me to you and you to me. Not knowing how you are is pretty awful, but I know it is so much worse for you, dear. My nose seems to be on the mend, after two weeks of hot fomentations. There was some infection in it and was so hard to get rid of.

[K.]

Sunday, April 26, 1942

Lots more rain. We have quite a few sick and the Japs will give us practically nothing to work with. Lots of promises but little action. Rations are pretty slim these days.

[At this point in the chronology, I will begin to integrate letters written from home to my dad, telling him of events at home. We hoped these stories would bring him comfort.—*Ed.*]

My dear Ken,

 After weeks and months of terrible anxiety, the worst we have ever experienced, it seems we can write and just hope that it reaches you some time, so you will know that day by day we have waited for some real news of just where you are and how things are going. I have been down two or three times and spent some time with May and Harvelyn and can truly say they have carried on bravely and have just lived from day to day waiting for news. Everyone is pretty well—Harvelyn and Katy were up and stayed the Easter holidays with us and we enjoyed them and they had a good time. You will get a surprise when the time comes that we have peace again and you can see for yourself what a fine big girl Harvelyn is. May has been very brave and has tried so hard to be bright through all the lonely and depressing weeks and months; thank goodness she is so comfortable and has so many good friends. We are getting nice spring weather; rather wet this week but everything looking lovely and green. Bob is busy as usual at the wholesale and at his garden and lawn in the evenings. We have not had our car out yet; restrictions on gas and tires are no very great hardship for us. I have my housecleaning almost done and I am sorry for it is real hard work, but one must clean up once in a while. I hear from Doris and Laurence* every week. They are well and the men at the university are taking a training course. I do not know yet, but I am hoping to go and see them some time this summer. Diane will soon have a birthday. They soon grow up, don't they? I am feeling better just now, but had a bad winter with one thing and another; that miserable rash was so bad for weeks.

Babe and Ken have been up to Brandon several times but I have not seen them. Mac McGregor is very sick; do not know how the poor fellow keeps going. Jess was down in Winnipeg for three weeks in charge of the hostess house at Osborne Barracks; she said she enjoyed it and it was good experience, only wishes she could get something permanent. Our town seems very busy and it is almost impossible to get a house of any kind; I think it might be a good time to sell this one.

Aunt Maggie has gone to Brantford for a visit. Uncle Hep died in December; also, Uncle Jim Sanderson died and their only son was lost in [the] Pearl Harbor disaster.

I am sure you will be getting word from May now and you will know what is going on in Winnipeg. Bob and I may go down in a week or two if we can arrange it. I will go down anyway and stay for a while.

We are so sorry that Louise (your sister) has been so miserable again and only

* My mother's sister and her husband.—*Ed.*

hope before long she will be better. If you could only know, Ken, how we long to hear some good news, everyone you know asks for you but we are trying to be hopeful and patient and trust before long to get good news.

[Bob]*

Sunday, May 3rd, 1942

My dearest Ken:

At last we have been told that we can write you a couple of letters and send a parcel. I have just sent my parcel off tonight and all I hope and pray is that you may receive both parcel and letters. We have not heard anything of you—my last word was a cable from you early in December, so you may know the unbearable anxiety we have been through. If we could just hear that you are safe and well it would be heaven. We just heard on Thursday that Col. Sutcliffe had died and we all feel so badly. I do hope and pray that you are well. There isn't a minute you are out of my thoughts.

Now to tell you the news that you want to know: we are both well, and you must not worry about us. I took Harvelyn to the doctor and had a thorough check

* Bob is Robert Riddell Dowling, my maternal grandfather.—*Ed*.

up last week. She had had two bad colds and I hadn't had her examined for a long time. Her blood count was normal and she was well in every way, so I felt relieved. You will also be glad to know that I had my eyes examined. Dr. Grieves said they were perfect and I did not need glasses, so evidently it isn't my eyes that cause these dreadful headaches.

I bought the radio for Harvelyn for Christmas and gave it to her from us and she was simply thrilled. I don't think we could have given her anything she would like better. It is in her room and she has it on all the time. This spring, I bought her a bicycle; she rides back and forth to school every day and gets such a lot of pleasure out of it. I am nervous, but every child has one. I had promised next Christmas I will give her a new wrist watch from us, I think; she is getting a little big for yours.

I hope the parcel I sent is all right—it was a little overweight, so I had to choose between taking out a shirt or a bar of washing soap. I took out the soap and sent you 3 shirts. The shirts will last longer and surely there will be soap you can use. It snowed today—think of it—in May and has been so cold, but the buds are all out and the hedges are green.

In your parcel: Father and Mother sent the running shoes and a long-sleeved shirt; Cliff sent the pipe; Mary and Jolly, the soap; and Doris and Laurence sent

$2 to get you something, so the pajamas are from them. They all send their very best love to you and pray that you are well. Harvelyn and Katy went up to Brandon for a week at Easter. I didn't go. They had a lovely time and felt so very grown up going off alone. Doris wants us to go down this summer, but we plan to stay here. I think I feel better at home. Louise has been sick again and is in a nursing home and is improving now. She went up with Mabel for Christmas, but came home soon after.

I have no maid now and am very tied up at nights. It keeps me busy, though, and that is good for me. I don't know whether to bother getting anyone for a while. It is rather nice to be alone except for not getting out at nights. Mother and Father came down at Christmas and I was glad they were here. I couldn't have gone there. What a lovely tray you gave me and how I love it. Please, God, we will have tea off it together one day not too far away. If you can write to me, be sure to tell me the things you need so that if we can send another box I will be able to send them. I would like to have put in another pair of shorts, but they weigh a lot so I will next time. Do you need a blanket and would you like heavy trousers? The nice hand-knitted socks are from your cousin, Mrs. Hathaway, in Detroit. I am going to the dentist tomorrow—Dr. Riley that used to live next door to us. That seems a long time ago. If only you could walk in the door—what a lot we have to talk about. But you must know that we are thinking of you always and praying for your safe return. I am wondering if you received any of the letters I wrote to you. I had two from you after you arrived. Harvelyn is going to write some in my next letter. I purposely left this late so that the news would be more up-to-date. We will write a couple more. Do be careful of yourself and keep well for our sake. We are hoping for good news of you one day, and until then, we live on hope. God bless you and keep you dear. Harvelyn and I both send all our love and our thoughts are with you always.

Molly

Sunday, May 3, 1942

Oceans of rain. The high rubber boots I bought are coming in very handy these days. No news, excepting what we see in the Jap papers and it is all in their favour. Yesterday everyone was ordered off the parade ground and eventually a Jap prince drove by in a car followed by scores of others. As nobody was interested, we all were reading or playing cards. They are a strange people! Two weeks from Thursday will be your birthday. I wish I could take you to dinner at the Alex or the Garry. I will be glad when we can eat a civilized meal again and order

CANADIAN NATIONAL
TELEGRAM

CANADIAN NATIONAL

D. E. GALLOWAY, ASSISTANT VICE PRESIDENT, TORONTO ONT.

CLASS OF SERVICE	SYMBOL
Full-Rate Message	
Day Letter	D L
Night Message	N M
Night Letter	N L

If none of these three symbols appears after the check (number of words) this is a full-rate message. Otherwise its character is indicated by the symbol appearing after the check.

T02GGX   74/73 2 EX DL GB STANDARD TIME

OTTAWA ONT 405PM MAY 9 1942

MRS MAY HARVELYN BAIRD   DEL 830PM
         1017   REPORT DELIVERY STE 1 DUBARRY APTS WINNIPEG MAN

2590 THE NAME OF YOUR HUSBAND MAJOR KENNETH GEORGE BAIRD OF THE WINNIPEG

GRENADIERS IS INCLUDED IN A SHORT LIST OF CANADIAN OFFICERS REPORTED

UNOFFICIALLY TO THE BRITISH AMBASSADOR AT CHUNGKING CHINA AS BEING HELD

PRISONER OF WAR AT NORTH POINT INTERNMENT CAMP HONGKONG STOP WHILE THE

LIST IS NOT OFFICIAL AND IS NOT COMPLETE WE ARE FORWARDING THIS INFORMATION

IN THE HOPE THAT IT WILL SOMEWHAT RELIEVE YOUR GREAT ANXIETY

            OFFICER I/C RECORDS

                    325PM

100

whatever we like best. For lunch today we had a small slice of bully beef, sour dough, bread and tea. Our meat issues are so rare the bully tasted great.

[K.]

Sunday, May 10, 1942

My dearest Ken,

I feel like a different person today, I can tell you—just 100 years younger. Yesterday I received a wire telling me you were safe. I can't tell you what I felt like when I read it. I just sat down and wept for sheer joy. It has been so dreadful not to know all these months. My phone has gone all day and everyone is so thrilled—several others heard too and my heart aches for those who didn't, although no doubt things are just starting to come through and they will hear soon. Harvelyn is so excited! This is Mother's Day, and Harvelyn spent her two weeks' allowance and bought me four lovely tulips. Wasn't it sweet of her, because she has to do it on her own, without her dad's help. Then to get my wire—wasn't that a wonderful present from you? I think no matter what we go through, the finest thing that life can offer is a husband (a good one) and children to think of you. We went to the memorial service this morning for Col.

Sutcliffe. My heart aches for poor Kay. It was very hard for us all. You will get an extra 100 cigs. from the Ladies' Auxiliary, which are to be distributed amongst your men. We are sending a lot of extra cigs. and I know how glad you will all be to have them. If you can write me I hope you are able to tell me what you need. I tried to put the things I thought most necessary in and had to keep it to 10 lbs., so it wasn't easy, but with three new shirts and your shorts, sweater, shoes, etc., you can manage nicely I think.

Doris Hanbury just phoned. She was so thrilled and said to give you her love. I'm just listening to Jack Benny. How I wish you could be here with me—never mind—we will hope it wouldn't be too long until we are together. I wired Doris, Margaret and Helen and phoned home and they were thrilled. Just see that you keep well now. I am just hoping that you will be able to send me a letter. Everything looks so green and fresh. It seems early for everything to be out. Last night Harvelyn slept at Katy's, so I went up to see Lucy and we both felt like setting off fireworks. We were so thrilled to know you were both safe, after all these months of hoping. Isn't it amazing what we can go through? Harvelyn wants to write one line.

Dear Daddy; we are so happy to know you are well. XOXO Harvelyn

I took her to a movie yesterday. She loves to do that and I won't let her go downtown alone. We got word when we got home and we were so excited we didn't have our dinner until 8:30. I still haven't any help and I am not going to bother getting anyone for a while. I don't know when we will be able to write you again but you will know that we are thinking of you always and I will write again just as soon as I am able. I hope your parcel and cigarettes and three letters arrive

Mrs. May (Molly) Harvelyn Baird.

safely. There are so many things I would like to say, but you will have to imagine them said. Thank God you are safe and I hope you keep well. Perhaps these will arrive near your birthday. We will be thinking of you and wishing you a happy day. Lots of love from us both, dear.

Molly

Sunday, May 10, 1942

Mother's Day. Have been wishing I could send you a message. There was a piece in the local paper copied from a Lisbon paper stating the Canadians are getting enough to eat, how our own trucks go out for food, how we have our own bake ovens, etc. As for our bake oven, our men built and experimented until they have one that works, but no thanks to Jap aid. We could really live well here if we could get the food to cook. Last night the mess steward gave us cheese sandwiches, jelly tarts, and cocoa about 10:00 p.m. We all nearly swooned. Unfortunately, it isn't likely to happen again as it was the last of the supplies he had and there wasn't enough to make a real meal out of it. Of course, we had bought these things ourselves. The Japs have told us we have sustained severe naval loss; they exaggerate like the devil so it may be we came off not too badly.

If we could only exchange letters, dearest, it would help so much. If I only knew you both are all right and well, and if I could only let you know that I am OK. I try to distribute smokes to the men as evenly as I can, but when my company numbers 140 I can't do it very often, and smokes mean so much. The boys are making sandals and all sorts of things to sell for cigarettes. I have a cribbage board, sandals and a cane made by my men, and they are beautifully made too. The sandals are comfortable and will save my shoes against the day we are released. A new pair through the canteen would cost $40 Hong Kong money, or 20 military yen, which would mean over $50 Canadian and poor leather at that.

Best love to you both,
Ken

Wednesday, May 13, 1942
One week tomorrow will be your birthday, Sweetheart. How I wish I could see you, talk to you and above all hold you in my arms and tell you the thousands of thoughts I have of you, but I suppose it will be a long time before I can do all these wonderful things—not too long I hope. We don't dare talk much of home,

we get too blue, and we all know the other fellow is in the same spot we are in, so we just think our thoughts and try not to get too far into the dumps. . . . we are having an awful lot of rain. Every day it simply pours, so that doesn't add anything to help along.

Last night the little beasts killed an old Chinaman right in front of our huts for walking on the wrong side of the road. They kicked his feet out from under him; he hit his head on the pavement, fracturing his skull. They left him there for two hours, then carted him off in a wheel barrow and dumped him in a vacant lot at the end of our camp. Delightful little beasts, aren't they?

We had a nice dinner tonight (it happens once in a while). We had a nice piece of steak, sweet potatoes, carrots, gravy, bread, stewed dates and tea. Our meals have improved so much since we started getting some pay. We buy all the extras that make the difference.

[K.]

Sunday, May 16, 1942

This is the first day without rain for three weeks so we have been airing our clothes and blankets all day long. Yesterday the Japs had two women tied to a lamp post all day long. They had shot the husband of the woman and tied the mother and daughter up . . . just because they were out after curfew.

[K.]

Thursday, May 21, 1942

Hello, Sweetheart,

   This is your birthday. I have been thinking of you all day long and wishing I could be with you or, second best, talk to you over long distance. I do hope that soon you will receive a letter or card. We hear they are going to let us write and receive mail—what a glorious day it will be when the first letters arrive. The two regiments, the Royal Rifles and W.G.s [Winnipeg Grenadiers], are putting in a large garden; there are about 60 men working on it. We hope for some good vegetables. We have company concerts each week, quiz contests, spelling matches, etc. They all keep the men interested and the prizes are cigarettes. I hand out about five cigarettes for each one I smoke and believe me it keeps us all broke trying to make the men's lives a little more livable. I am as blue as the devil today, I miss you both so much. Even if we didn't do so much over here, the Japs respect the Canadians as fighters and say we put up a darned good show for our money.

This will stand us in good store when they crack up next year—I hope. Do you remember the day war was declared? We were listening to the radio in Brandon and you asked me when I thought it would finish. I said November 1943. Well, that is 18 months away, and I still think it will be that long. What a glorious day it will be when we know it is all over.

[K.]

Sunday, May 24, 1942

Hello, Dearest,

I wonder what you are doing today. It will be a long weekend with people away and all that. We will have an extra long weekend—behind a wire fence. Yesterday the Japs ordered us out on parade and insisted upon us signing a form that we would not try to escape. Everyone signed it under protest. The Col. in charge of prison camps spoke to us in Japanese. He had an interpreter that had the most objectionable manner. We all thought plenty, as he talked. They were asked if they would sign such a paper if they were in our place. They said yes, but wouldn't consider it binding, as the Japanese are Sons of Heaven and only answer to their Heaven-born Emperor. They said we would keep our word if we signed, being Canadians. The swine. They have the Huns' idea of signing anything, it means nothing.

One of the most interesting and surprising things in this camp is the Handicraft Guild. The first exhibition was held yesterday and was a revelation to me. Some of the carvings and woodwork are really wonderful: rings made of silver coins, gloves, socks, mitts knitted on needles made of wood, drawings, etchings and carvings, inlaid cigarette cases, boxes, canes and dozens of things. There were over 60 entries, some of the drawings made by a man in the Rifles that can neither read nor write. There is a lot of sickness in the lines. The doctors are quite worried as the cholera season is approaching. Yesterday we were served as a vegetable boiled cucumbers. They were awful, simply terrible in fact, but darned good raw. Why they cooked them I don't know, but they experiment all the time and usually hit things right.

John Crawford and I were speaking about some of the food two of the officers left on their plate. We recalled the days at Shamshuipo. One forgets the hungry past, but the look in everyone's eyes at that time will, I think, remain in our minds for a long time. The sun is shining this morning, we have only had about

宣誓書

AFFIDAVIT

I hereby swear that I shall not make

any attempt to escape whilest I am a prisoner of The Imperial

Japanese Army.

Dated this 15/7/ day of   17th year of Showa.

THE COMMANDER-IN-CHIEF
HONG KONG PRISONERS OF WAR CBMP
HONG KONG

(Signed) _____

An example of the affidavit signed by Hong Kong prisoners of war.

110

three days of it in over a month. The rain has really been heavy and lots of it. I am reading *Nanking Road* and find it quite interesting. I wish I had a letter from you today to read instead of this book.

[K.]

Thursday, May 28, 1942

Hello, Dearest,

Nearly another month gone by and that much nearer home. We have had three days of sunshine and heat. It looks as though we will find this camp a bit of a hell hole when summer really arrives. Everyone is dreading the sickness the doctors expect to encounter. I have nearly half of my company on the sick list, 61 out of 141, and more going every day. Dysentery, beriberi, and general rundown conditions all due to lack of food of the proper kind. Everyone has a bad skin rash or boils or ulcers, due to a lack of vitamins. Yesterday the Japs made an issue to us of one small face towel, one cake of soap, one toothbrush and some tooth powder, and four packets of toilet paper. They have decided we have been too well fed so they are cutting our rations by 20 per cent. The men will now have one bun for lunch. They are cutting out the tea issue altogether. They won't give the doctors any supplies to treat the sick. They come around and listen to the doctors' pleas for supplies and do damn all about it.

Last night they caught a Chinese man and every little while they beat hell out of him. We could hear his cries all through the night. At Bowen Road Hospital they caught three Chinese men that had been looting. They tortured them all night long, then covered them with gasoline and set them on fire. Poisonous little b——, aren't they? We have been given prisoner of war numbers that we have to wear sewn on our shirts on our right chest. My number is 4446, so now all they need to do is take our finger prints and take our pictures to make real convicts of us. The Col. in charge of prison camps told the commanding officers that only by kind permission of the Imperial Jap government were we to be treated as officers, but really we aren't officers but just prisoners of war. Nice fellow, what!

At last we are going to be allowed to write home. The first mail leaves on June 6. It will be wonderful to sit down and actually write you, dearest, hoping it will reach you. What they will allow us to say we don't know, but the chance to write is really wonderful.

[K.]

112

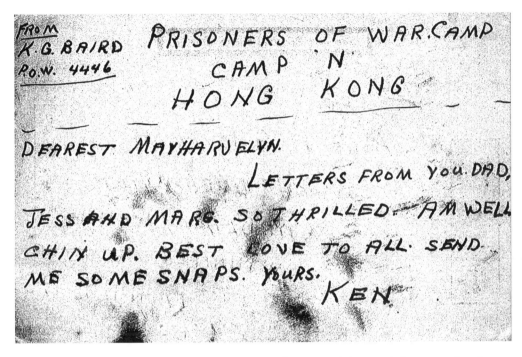

One of several postcards sent by Major Baird. Most of the mail that circulated to and from the camp was sent to Japan to be examined by censors.

Saturday, May 30, 1942

We have just finished our monthly mess meeting and there is the usual Sat. night concert on the square. It is also a beautiful moonlit night. How I wish we could be enjoying it together. We are all so excited about writing home, our first letter is to be handed in by the third of June. It will be a hard letter to write as we are only allowed 200 words and that doesn't allow one to say hardly anything at all and we all have so much to tell you about. It will be prosy and inadequate I am sure. Sickness is mounting. I have over 50 per cent of my men on the sick list and the food isn't as good as it was for a little while. More later, Sweetheart.

[K.]

Friday, July 3, 1942

Today we had an inspection by Col. Tokunaga, the Jap officer in charge of all prison camps in this area. With him were two Red Cross representatives, Swiss or Portuguese. We just learned our casualty list hasn't been sent. Damn their hides. All this time I have been hoping you would know I am all right and now

114

you haven't had one word. I can just imagine the hundreds of times you have been asked if you have had any word from me and your answer would be *no*.

[K.]

Sunday, July 5, 1942

Yesterday our second broadcast was given. It is recorded on a recorder sent to Tokyo and presumably sent from there. I hope they have gone. The interpreter told Cols. Price and Trist that the first one had been sent over the air so if that is true you will have heard that I am all right. Since 6:30 a.m. it has rained like the devil. We have had feet of rain since coming into this camp. There are millions of rumours flying around about moving us.

[K.]

Instructions given by Colonel Y. Noguchi,
Superintendent of the Chosen War Prisoners' Camp*

September, 1942

(It is requested that you should preserve these papers after having read through.)

I am Colonel Y. Noguchi, Superintendent of the Chosen War Prisoners' Camp. Receiving you here, I should like to give necessary instructions to you all.

I hope you will consider how this Greater East Asia war happened. Nippon's desire for peaceful settlement arising from the conciliatory spirit, rejected by America and Britain in order to attain their ambitious demand in East Asia. Finally, they overwhelmed Nippon, the important defenser of Asia, to the extent that they dared to resort to violence of economic disruption.

Promoting Chinese internal confusion and increasing military preparation on all sides of Nippon Empire to challenge us, thus the very existence of our nation being in danger, we stood up resolutely with unity of will, strong as iron, under

* This document is a verbatim transcript of the original.—*Ed*.

116

the name of Jenno (Emperor) for the emancipation of the nations and elimination of evil sources in East Asia.

The rise or fall of our Empire that has the glorious history and the progress or decline depend upon the present war. Firm and unshakable is our national resolve, that we should quash our enemy, the U.S.A. and the Britain.

Heaven is always on the side of Justice. Within ten days after the War Declaration, our Navy and naval Air Forces annihilated both the American Pacific fleet and the British Far Eastern fleet; within a few months, American and British long-established Army, Navy and Air Bases were crushed by our Army and Army Air Forces; and now, tide turning in our favour, all parts of regions linked with Burma, Java, and Wake Island have already been occupied by us, and the inhabitants there are rejoicing in cooperation with us for the construction of new Asia. And now these above facts have induced the Indian rebellion and Australia come to a crisis of capture. Afterwards, belligerents sent their aircrafts and fleets for the rescue, but every time they were sunk to the bottom or destroyed and repulsed, thus the total damages came up to 2,801 vessels and 4,000 aircrafts.

I think these war results do not signify the inferior power of our enemy but rather owe to our absolute indomitable power—that is to say the power protected by Kami (heaven). Wherever Nippon Army and Navy advance, Jenyu

Shinjo (special providential help) always follows; you should recognize the fact and consider the reasons.

Nippon Army and Navy are under the Imperial Command of Jenno (Emperor) who is the personification of Kami (God) so that the Imperial troops are to be called the troops of God. Now you have become war prisoners because of struggling against Kami no-gun (God's army) and now you are convinced of fearfulness to the marrow and become aware of unsavoury results. What do you think of this?

However you have lost fighting strength now, you once fought fiercely against us. Judging from this fact some of you will hold hostile feeling again at us in your hearts that can never be permission. Accordingly, we will punish you if you act against our regulations, for instance the non-fulfillment of regulations, disobedience, resistance, and escape (even an attempt to do so) are understood as manifestations of hostility.

I kindly request that you must be cautious not spoiling yourselves by punishment. But on the other hand, with Nippon warrior's forgiveness, I express respect to your faithfulness to your country and fulfillment of your duty, and feel pitiful for your capitulations after exhaustion.

You should reflect on yourselves. According to the extent of your malice feeling we also put certain limit on our freedom you enjoy or severity and lenity of your treatment.

Paroles is of use as a proof of wiping away your hostility. I am regretful to say that those refused to swear will be treated as persons of enemy character, will be placed under restraint regarding maintenance of honour, protection of your persons, and must endure pain in compensation of hostility.

The details of concrete outline of style of daily life are defined in the "regulations regarding to daily life;" you should put them into practice strictly after reading over them.

Prejudice against labour and grumbling over food, clothing and housing are strictly prohibited, because the change in your daily life and custom are inevitable under present war situation.

Closing my instructions, I advise you all to find interest and anxiety in your forthcoming daily life by acting according to the Imperial military discipline.

Dearest Ken,

Here I am again! I'm going to print this letter—I wish I had a typewriter. You can hardly believe it, but we had snow here today. It did not stay, but it made us think that winter was just around the corner. I am afraid I will have to buy Harvelyn a new fall coat. Her brown one is too small—she can't move her arms and the sleeves are short. After all, I got it three years ago now and she has grown a lot in that time. She has shot up this past year. She has joined the YMCA for dancing and gym and is very thrilled. She is really lovely looking and I think will be a very pretty girl. She is beginning to be aware of herself. Puts cream on her face at night and hopes that she is not going to have your freckles. She likes her school and seems to be doing well.

Mr. Leech has been up with Father and stayed nearly three weeks. He phoned me and said Father had tripped over the hose and broken three ribs. This happened three weeks ago and he didn't want me to know, or Mother. Mother is still with Doris and having a lovely visit. Father wouldn't want her to worry. Mother said she had written you.

We read in the papers that you had received our mail and some food parcels.

We were so thrilled to hear that. Hope you also received the cigarettes we sent. I will be glad when you receive our boxes.

I went to see Louise the other day. She is much better, but is still in the nursing home. I think it is the best place for her, as she gets the care she needs. Margaret writes me sermons every so often. We are going to have our bathroom, kitchen and all our white woodwork painted so it will be nice and clean. I have been making a little jelly and pickle. We don't need so very much but is nice to have some.

Lucy and Mrs. Sutcliffe are coming over here tomorrow night. I am still alone and do not intend to get anyone. I can get a girl to come in evenings when I want to go out and that is all I want.

I wonder if we will get another letter from you soon! I hope one before Xmas.

Sept. 27—On Friday I had been out to tea and when I got home, Father was here. He had motored down to spend my anniversary with me and I was shocked—he is so thin and in dreadful pain with his broken ribs. He never should have motored. He had to drive with one hand and is suffering so much. I will be glad when Mother is home. He left just after dinner today. I am very worried about him. I have been thinking of you today, and you have probably been thinking of me. Mother, Doris and L. have sent me a wire, and Rita and Cliff sent lovely flowers. They are so good to me. Harvelyn bought me candy so you see I wasn't neglected. I wish you were here to celebrate. A long time, but we seem to have spent a lot of that time apart. We will make up for it some day. Half a world between us, but I am so thankful we are both in the world. Good night, dear, and a happier anniversary next year!

Love,
Molly

Saturday, September 26, 1942

The past two months have just been the same old routine, the occasional work parties and the two daily parades, so I haven't written anything. Here we are, on the move again. We are being moved back to Shamshuipo to the same barracks we came to just after we surrendered. We have been nine months at North Point camp. We have done everything to make it as comfortable as possible with nothing to work with. The most surprising thing has been the ingenious way the men have developed and fashioned scraps of things into useful articles. The Japs are moving some of the Imperial troops to Japan to work. They have moved about

2,000, and more to go. I wonder if we will be sent. When we came over to Shamshuipo I had to leave a very comfortable bed made of rice sacks behind. A real Beauty Rest bed. I bought a folding deck chair that I am now sitting in as I scribble this. We had a long day when we moved, up at 5:00 a.m. and left there about noon. We were all loaded down with our prize possessions. If ever you saw a parade of the lame, the sick, and the halt, ours was it. We should have at least 150 more of them in the hospital. Dysentery, beriberi, mouth and eye trouble, and pellagra—all these are due to lack of proper rations. We can't get any anti-toxin for the Dip [diphtheria] and we are in a position where we will lose a lot of men unless something happens and supplies are brought in. Already in the Imperial lines there have been a lot of deaths; there are over 500 in the camp hospitals out of a total of about 3,500. We have been here only a few days and have had one or two funerals each day. One of our men died of diphtheria. Every day sees a lot more go to hospital, either to isolation or to the Dip and dysentery wards. Over 150 now in isolation and over 600 in hospital. All told, about a sixth of the camp. The Japs have ruled that everyone not admitted to hospital must be on the morning and evening parade, so we see men being carried on the backs of others and on stretchers too weak to stand or walk themselves. They look like walking skeletons. I have forgotten whether I have written about being in Bowen Road Hospital for 16 days with dysentery. I was lucky and got it cleared up in about 10 days. I just got back to North Point before coming to Shamshuipo. Yesterday Jack Bailie and I took a work party to the new airport at Kai Tak. From this camp there have been from 600 to 800 men per day going. At present they are moving a small hill about 350 ft. long by 250 wide and 50 high. This is being done by pick and shovel, so it will be a long time before it is levelled. The Japs have demolished a part of the city housing about 100,000 people and covering an area about two square miles. They have just turned them out and are tearing down their homes and blocks. True, a lot of them are just hovels, but homes nevertheless.

The routine of our life here, day in and day out, varies very little. Reveille at 4:30 a.m., breakfast at 5:00. Parade falls in about 5:30 and is checked and then marched over to the parade ground where the Japs check them. We wait for an hour usually for the ferry, then a trip down the harbour that takes an hour and twenty minutes to where we disembark at the Kai Tak dock, then about a half mile's walk to the airport where the men go to work. They work until 11:30 and then break off for lunch, which consists of a quarter loaf of dry bread and water to drink. At 12:30 they are back at work and carry on until 3:00 p.m., when they have a half hour's break. The men are given five little candies and two cigarettes. The candies are like the red raspberries we put in a youngster's stocking at

Christmas. They go back to work until 5:15, when they turn in their picks and shovels and then line up for counting again. They sometimes count the men eight times in one day. Suspicious bunch, what! We usually pull away from the dock on our homeward trip about 6:00 and by the time we arrive back in camp and are counted again and dismissed it is getting on towards 8:00 p.m.

The men rush for a shower and supper, or just supper according to the man, and try to get rested to start the same damn thing all over again the next morning. This goes on seven days each week. In our whole battalion we have one h— of a time to turn out 225 men and a good part of them aren't fit to go. I hope when and if you ever read this, Molly, that you won't think all the reams I have written are because I am feeling sorry for myself, because I am not. I have been one of the few lucky ones in that I haven't had any of the diseases, excepting dysentery, that most of them have had and are still suffering from, and I do feel darn lucky and thankful. I must be a tough nut, but mustn't start crowing.

Our rations are slightly better but can be vastly improved upon. Our main diet is rice in the morning and at night; at noon, two slices of dried bread and rice coffee, a God-awful drink. Someone brought some garlic in to camp so we rub a bit on the bread—that is, some of us—and at least it tastes different, and that is something. We got an issue of tobacco yesterday from the Japs. It looks like stable sweepings and smells and tastes like hell. We all save our cigarette butts and smoke them. I tried mixing a little of the issue tobacco but nearly passed out after a few puffs, so now I pour boiling water on the tobacco and drain the juice off. It is a wonderful thing for B-bugs. They just curl up and die and we have an inexhaustible number to work on.

[K.]

Sunday, October 4, 1942

Yesterday, 18 new cases of Dip developed in our camp of about 1,500. It is really awful here. Several hundred cases of Dip and carriers and not one thing to work with. The MOs are nearly crazy. Two more deaths yesterday, and lots more to come by the looks of things.

[K.]

Saturday, October 10, 1942

We have now been here [Shamshuipo] two weeks today and are gradually getting settled. We have so little to work with, as I have mentioned before. There isn't a window or door in any of our huts, so what it will be like when the cold weather comes, I hate to think. In one of these rambles on paper I mentioned the Chinese having taken all windows and doors. The fact that wood sells by the pound caused them to take every piece of furniture, doors, window sills, and all else they could tear out. We are starting to dig up pieces of corrugated iron to make doors of, and the windows in the huts occupied by the Imperials are bricked up about three-quarters of the way and the rest is open. It has been raining most of the day, with a strong wind blowing, and although the thermometer registers 78, we are darned chilly; this wind comes down from the hills and we have no heat of any kind. We haven't had any since we were captured. I can just imagine how an open fireplace would seem like a bit of heaven. Today is the first day since we arrived that we haven't had a funeral in this camp. There have been from one to three funerals each day, nearly all the deaths from Dip. It is pretty ghastly, there are 18 new cases today. We have a new hospital just opened where Dip carriers are isolated. There are 80 carriers there to date and more going every day. We have a dysentery hospital where there are over 300, and in all the camp about 500 or 600 are in hospital for all diseases.

About 10 days ago they moved about 1,800 Imperial troops from here. They said they were taking them to Japan. In yesterday's paper it was reported the boat was torpedoed with a heavy loss of life. The Americans are blamed for the torpedoing. There isn't much to write about these days—just routine jobs and things in general at a fairly low ebb with all this sickness, and there are hundreds of pitiful cases. I can just imagine a lot of old young men arriving home. There are several boys here that aren't yet 20 that look 50 years old and walk like men of 80. I am not fooling when I write this either.

[K.]

Sunday, October 11, 1942

Six more deaths during the last 12 hours, has been raining all day, have been busy building a new bed. The one I now have, an iron barrack bed, is like sleeping on a rock pile. I have just read a bit of poetry that fits this place most aptly: "Morning never comes too soon, I can face the afternoon / But Oh! those lonely nights." It is nearly time for our evening parade. Everyone will get wet and stay so all night. Cheerio for now, Sweetheart.

Ken

Friday, October 17, 1942

I took the funeral party out today. We buried five more Canadians, three Royal Rifles and two Grenadiers. One was Eric Eastholm from my company. He had been with me since the war started. Just recently we have been able to buy—*buy*, mind you—some anti-toxin for the Dip. cases, but not one-tenth enough. The camp have spent hundreds of yen, put up by all the officers to buy this anti-toxin. There were five million units in the colony here, so someone is making a nice bit of graft at the expense of many of our men's lives. The total lack of medicine and antiseptics for treatment makes one sick at heart. I have been so fortunate in not being sick or having any of these terrible diseases. The Japs yesterday lined up all the hospital orderlies and asked the orderlies—who, by the way, have volunteered to go into the sick ward where they have never had any experience at all, where they are more than likely to contract either Dip. or dysentery and work under conditions that would make a trained nurse or orderly sick—the Jap medical officer asked all the orderlies that felt they were doing their very best to take one step forward. They all stepped forward. They all had their faces slapped by an NCO of the Japs, and the Jap officer slapped Major Crawford's face and told them they weren't half trying or there wouldn't be half so many deaths. The poisonous little beasts, they withhold all the medical supplies or sell them to us and then treat the medical staff in that way.

[K.]

Sunday, October 18, 1942

Another death today. Major Bailie's Coy took the party out.

[K.]

Sunday, October 25, 1942

Ten months today since our capture and hurrah! Twelve of our planes came over and dropped a few bombs on the docks. Oh! Molly, they sounded just great; it means we haven't been forgotten after all these long months. A cheer went up from all our camp. There is a big fire down near the docks. The Jap guards are tearing around all over camp, ordering everyone into their huts and setting up machine guns in case we are tempted to start something. The planes arrived at

3:45. Our planes have moved on and now the Jap planes are gathering around. This has proven a great boon to us all: we have something to talk about that is really true. Rumours aren't worth a damn.

[K.]

At 1:30 a.m. our planes came back and dropped some more bombs. We were tickled to death; the Japs were running around camp and greatly excited. Yesterday we were all ordered into our huts. The Japs were throwing their weight around quite a bit for an hour, so now we are looking forward to their next move (I mean our side). We have three dates, all on the 25th: I left home on the 25th of Oct., surrendered on Dec. 25 and have had our first air raid by our side on Oct. 25—one year to the day from leaving home. So I hope by next Christmas we will all be free and at home with the only people in the world that matter—our wives and daughters—meaning you and Harvelyn.

Three weeks ago the Japs told us lots of Red Cross parcels had arrived and would be delivered in a few days. Nothing more has been heard of them. They have started delivering some of the food that came in on the R.C. [Red Cross] boat. They are delivering to the Indians first flour and ghi oil. It is like beef drippings. We have received some of the ghi oil and it tastes darn good as we haven't had any fats for months. We have had peanut oil to fry things in, but our systems are starved for meat fats and it will do us all a lot of good. The lack of necessary food has left the men in such a pitiful state, nothing I could write would convey anything near the true picture of things. On top of everything else the boys have what they call electric feet. They burn and ache terribly and when you see men sitting and holding their feet, rocking back and forth and crying like a child, well it must be hell and is pretty *awful* to see. There are supposed to be large quantities of medical supplies downtown, but we have never received them or had one thing to help. Our deaths from Dip. and dysentery have been pretty awful, as many as five at a time. I had three in my company in three days. Dip. seems to be letting up a little, but dysentery and pellagra are getting worse and our last few deaths have been caused by them. The Japs have forbidden us to go to the latrines after lights out. The results are pretty awful. The Japs have taken away all the old guards and have brought a bunch of youngsters from Formosa. I hope things are taking a turn our way. The lack of news is the hardest thing to put up with. If I could only get a message from you, Sweetheart, and get one to you, life would be a lot better and time wouldn't seem quite so long. Bye for now.

Best love,
Ken

Friday, November 13th, 1942.

Dear Ken,

I know the girls have been writing you but thought you might like to hear from the old man.

Mother had a nice trip East and had a lovely visit with Doris. May and Harvelyn were up this summer and we had a good time. I have had three or four shoots this fall, the first in four years, and enjoyed them very much. Had a nice bag of twenty mallards on my last outing. The lake was frozen over and we had to depend on stray birds flying over the ice. I was in Winnipeg for your anniversary and had a nice time with May and Harvelyn. Harvelyn has grown so tall, nearly as tall as her mother.

We have had an early winter. I think the snow is here to stay. Jess is with us just now as they are winterizing her office. The men are on the road and expect to finish the end of this month.

Miss Potter, from the office, sends her love and that is something as she is a very popular young lady. Has a different escort to dinner about four times a week, so you will realize sending her love is not to be taken lightly.

We had a nice crop on the farm this year.

Your old friend Archie Campbell is in hospital and in very poor shape. Mr. Creelman is well and wishes to be remembered to you.

I am glad to know that you are being so well looked after and hope you will take the best care of yourself.

Love from us all,
R. R. Dowling.

Sunday, November 22, 1942

Both yesterday and today have been clear and warm after three or four days of wet and cold weather. Last Tuesday I took the work party out. It had been raining during the night and was cloudy and chilly. We got up about 4:15 a.m., had breakfast at 5:15, and all the men fell in on the parade ground at 6:15 and waited until nearly 7:00 for the ferry to come for us. We got to the place we work and it started to rain, so we got under cover in some mat sheds and were finally told to get ready to return to camp. We left at 10:30 and marched back, taking about an hour. We sent about 70 back by truck as they were unable to walk. The men are in awful shape, yet we have to turn out a definite number on each parade and consequently have to send about a quarter of our men that should be in hospital and in bed. At the end of August, a Red Cross ship brought in a supply of food and other things. Yesterday the first lot arrived in camp: bully beef, raisins, dried pears, and cocoa. How we enjoyed a bit of bully last night. It is the first meat to arrive in camp in over six months; consequently, the men have been suffering from all manner of sickness, electric feet, and ulcers such as I never thought possible. Malnutrition has run rampant. Dysentery and diphtheria have taken a lot of lives—all needlessly. Clothing and shoes are terribly scarce, yet plenty arrived on the Red Cross ship. Medicine can be had by buying it and there was enough on the island to look after everyone for two to three years. One can't help feeling bitter at the little ——s. The compradore brought us in some eggs at 30 yen each. That is about 85 cents Canadian per egg, so for breakfast I had a boiled egg, rice, sweetsauce (not so good, the sauce), toast, which we made on a toaster Jack Bailie and I made (the pride of our section of the mess), and tea. A darn good meal, all centred on the egg. You have no idea just what an egg means to us and how wonderful it tastes.

Ken

Wednesday, November 25, 1942, 2:30 p.m.

Eleven months ago at this hour, I wouldn't have given very much for our chances of getting out of the house we were in alive. Lordy, how they were plastering us. But all that I have written about before—but dates mean a lot when we reminisce. Since the Red Cross boxes arrived with food, we have been getting meals that resemble slightly the menu of a white man. Last night we had rice (always); baked beans; a slice of bully beef; a sweet potato, boiled then fried in peanut oil after being dipped in a batter; and for dessert, raisin pie and tea. Doesn't that sound just like a banquet? Well it tasted darn good to us anyway. There has been a lot of air activity by the Japs. The past few days they must have been expecting an air raid because they have had about a dozen fighters flying around all day long from dawn until dusk. They look and behave like darn good planes, too. Everyone is sleeping this afternoon. Believe it or not I can't sleep very often;

I get all I can absorb during the nights. They turn the lights off at 8:00 p.m. and so we sit in the dark and then go to bed about 9:30. So by 5:30 a.m. I am slept out and just lie and wait until it is time to get up.

Yesterday five more of my men went into the Dip. isolation hospital as carriers. The doctors are getting it more or less under control now, but dysentery is still pretty bad. It is heart-breaking to see the condition of the men. Generally speaking, they are all old men—thin as a rail and about enough energy left to move about—and we have to send them out on working parties. The Japs are great taskmasters and darn well see the work is done or someone gets slapped around. I will be glad when our turn comes to do some slapping. I hope we are not too soft-hearted with them, they are just savages and nothing else.

Ken

Friday, November 27, 1942

Just had word from the hospital that Capt. Terry, our paymaster, died on the 13th of diphtheria. He went in on the 10th and just passed out. Also Lt. Harper, one of my Coy officers, died about three weeks ago with it. The usual funeral seems to be taking place every day or two. We had one today. We have had two deaths of men who volunteered to go into our Dip. ward as orderlies. They contracted it and passed on. They should be honoured in some way for their service and work.

At noon today the air raid alarm went off and the Japs were racing around ordering everyone into their huts, but nothing ever came of it, darn it. What do you think, dearest? We have just been told that all the letters we wrote home are still in Tokyo. Damn their measly hides. We got some comfort out of thinking you would have at least a couple, and we also heard the casualty list hasn't gone either. I think it is criminal that they should act that way. They are savages at heart but think themselves the chosen people and most god-like—like hell they are.

[K.]

Thursday, December 10, 1942

One year ago today we were in the third day of the war. I was just beyond Wong Nai Chong Gap at Tylam Huts. It rained all day and was beastly cold, and the cold I had was getting the upper hand of me. Col. Sutcliffe came over to see me and took me off to put me in hospital as I had a pretty high temp. However, I went to an advanced dressing station and they gave me some pills that brought my temp. down so I beat it out of the station when the MOs weren't around and went back to my Coy.

Today it is cold and windy—darn cold, in fact. On Nov. 30 we were issued with Red Cross parcels with *food* in them. I am sure none of you at home could ever realize just what these parcels meant to us. Mine was packed in London last June. They arrived here the end of August and have been held for over two months before being distributed. We had begun to think they were a myth. However, they arrived and mine had the following items in it: two slabs of sugar, one bar of chocolate, one box of lime drops, a packet of tea, a tin of marmalade pudding (darn good too!), a tin of cheese (small), pineapple plum jam, a tin of tomatoes, a tin of gelatine (like bologna sausage), a half-pound tin of bacon (haven't tried it yet, am saving it to celebrate with—unless I get too hungry some day), a half-pound tin of margarine, one tin Nestlé's milk (worth its weight in gold to us), a tin of steak and vegetables, and a tin of biscuits. And besides this there has been bully beef and meat and vegetables in tins, so we have been eating somewhat better since the first of the month, and the boys are showing a little improvement on account of the extra diet. We have lost so many men from malnutrition, and our unit is made up principally of old young men. It is awful to see them, and since it has turned cold it hasn't helped much.

When we moved out of these barracks one year ago they were in good repair; when we came back three weeks later on Dec. 30 the Chinese had looted the place, taking out all the windows and doors, so you can imagine just how cold and drafty it is. Ten days ago I started bricking up all the windows in my two company huts and scrounged sheet metal and a couple of old doors to make doors of. I have now the two warmest huts in the lines, and the men are surely glad of it, but I had the devil's own time to get them to work on the huts. Then we fixed up the windows in our own part of our hut, and we are as comfortable as we can hope to be. We are only warm when we are in bed. It is always cold and raw, and that is not so very pleasant. If we could only have a fire to really toast ourselves once in a while, it would help a lot.

A few days ago they brought in some summer underwear and a sort of pullover jerkin. It is warm and most useful. There are rumours that there is to be another parcel for Christmas. I hope so, it will help a lot. We have another funeral today. One of the men died yesterday of pellagra. . . .

[K.]

Five more shopping days to Christmas. How I wish I could be with you, Sweetheart, to help do the many things that have to be done—going down with Harvelyn to do her shopping, secrets galore, and all kinds of hiding places that would be taboo for all of us. This will be my third Christmas away from you, Sweetheart, and that is just three too many. I hope by next year we will all be together and never miss another one for at least 30 years. By that time I will be long overdue for planting. We are planning our Christmas meals here also. We are hoping to have, as an extra special treat for breakfast, porridge, fried eggs, toast and coffee. I have saved my can of bacon that I got in my Red Cross parcel to have a real binge. We are trying to get enough ducks for our Christmas dinner. What else we may have depends on what the Japs will let us bring in. They—the Japs—say we will have a surprise for Christmas, but what it may be we have no idea. Rumours have it we are to get another Red Cross parcel. I hope so, they are really priceless. We have also saved a half pound of margarine, a tin of cheese (4 oz.) and a tin of marmalade. I hope they increase the bread issue for that day, as we only receive one bun a day and that doesn't go very far. We are having a visit from the International Red Cross representative today. I hope they give him a chance to really see the conditions that prevail in this camp. It would open his eyes and make him realize how the little brown Bs have held up medical supplies. Will tell you all about our Christmas festivities later. Bye-bye for now.

Best love,
Ken

Thursday, December 24, 1942

Dearest Molly and Harvelyn,

I have been fighting off a bout of the blues for the past two weeks and today they descended in full force, but then I soon found it to be a bad way to spend a day. I cheered myself up by thinking that I really am darn lucky. I am alive, my health is OK, I am getting enough to eat. In fact, the meals are awfully good in comparison to what they have been for nine months of the twelve that we have been prisoners. Then one can't go around with a dismal look on one's face, especially when about three-quarters of the men are sick and looking darn bad. That is one thing that is far from cheerful. What really made me feel blue was the fact that I couldn't be home with you and Harvelyn. Three Christmases are too many to miss by at least three, and then not being able to write or cable you or hear from you—well, Dearest, it makes it sort of tough, but then everyone else is in the same boat here so we don't let on to each other how we feel very often. I had your pictures, the snaps I carried in the case Marg gave me, and the fellows said I was darn lucky to have them as they lost all theirs. I take them out so often and hope that you both are well and happy and doing the things that help make each day pass in a pleasant way, to say the least. I only hope you have had some word of us to relieve you of some worry.

Today we received the first news of Canada. It came through the Red Cross. Each man received an envelope with two Christmas trees on it and printed on it was a greeting from the people of Canada and it held a 10 yen note. You haven't any idea how the envelope cheered everyone up, the first we have had since leaving home. And of course the 10 yen, the first money some of the men have had in one year's time, was a perfect godsend. I took mine and bought cigarettes for the NCOs and men of my company, and have one yen left. It was the only thing I could buy that they would appreciate. Then the Officers' Mess gave each NCO and man a half pound of salt. Doesn't that sound like a screwy thing to give for a Christmas remembrance? Well! there wasn't a thing they would have liked better—excepting to be on their way home. So many came to me and said it was the one and only thing they wanted or needed most. I hope this Christmas Eve you both are just as happy and excited as can be and that you have bought yourselves something you really would like to have as a present from me. I miss like the very devil not being around to help get cards away, wrap up parcels, and have hiding places for things, and seeing Punkle do her things up and the excitement of it all. The moon is full and I made a wish to it in the middle of the night. I hope that in some mysterious way it reached you both in your dreams. Good night, Sweethearts.

With all my love and best wishes for your happiness for tomorrow and all the tomorrows that will come for the rest of your lives,

Ken & Daddy

Friday, December 25, 1942

A very Merry Christmas to you, Molly and Harvelyn. Last night some of the officers came into our room and we sang Christmas carols and acted out the fool and sang all sorts of crazy songs. I am sure anyone hearing us would think we were on an awful binge but not a drop of anything did we have, darn it! Some of us went to the midnight Communion service and then got to bed about 1:00 a.m., the latest I have been up since leaving home. Fourteen months ago today we left home, and what a long, long time it has been. Never having received one letter or word of any kind makes it that much tougher. I only hope I get all the letters that are somewhere between here and home. One year ago today at this time we were on the receiving end of a terrific shelling, bombing, and trench mortar and machine gun barrage. The house we were in was simply dancing from the explosions and how it stood up is a mystery.

Well, Sweetheart, we had a wonderful breakfast. Porridge and milk, two fried eggs, coffee, and a bread bun with a little jelly. The eggs tasted like a million. I will tell you how the rest of the day passes. I will write some more tomorrow.

So again Merry Christmas, Sweethearts, and all my love,

Ken & Daddy

Sunday, December 27, 1942

Haven't had a chance to settle down to write anything since Christmas. Our lunch on Christmas was a bully beef patty, french-fried sweet potatoes, bread and tea. We then went down to the kitchens and helped serve the men's Christmas dinner. They had a darn good meal too: rice, a whole sweet potato (roasted), a whole tin of meat and vegetables, a Christmas pudding, an 8 oz. roll of bread, four cigarettes and tea. A darn good meal too. I left just as they were about finished as it was my bath day. Oh yes! We have two hot baths a week and I would rather miss any-

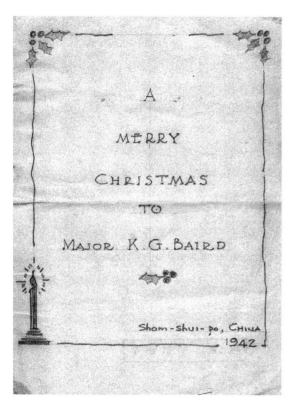

A

MERRY

CHRISTMAS

TO

MAJOR. K.G. BAIRD

Sham-Shui-po, CHINA
1942

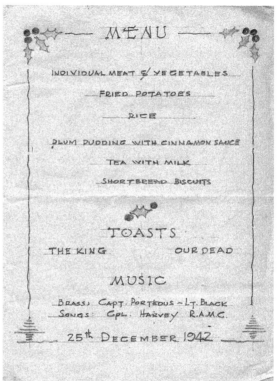

MENU

INDIVIDUAL MEAT & VEGETABLES

FRIED POTATOES

RICE

PLUM PUDDING WITH CINNAMON SAUCE

TEA WITH MILK

SHORTBREAD BISCUITS

TOASTS

THE KING   OUR DEAD

MUSIC

BRASS: CAPT. PORTEOUS – LT. BLACK
SONGS: CPL. HARVEY R.A.M.C.

25th DECEMBER 1942

<OFFICERS>

· OFFICERS ·
IN ATTENDANCE

Lt-Col. G. Trist	Major H.W. Hook
Major E.H. Hodkinson	", J.A. Baillie
" K.G. Baird	Capt. J.A. Norris
Capt. R.W. Philip	" E.B. Walker
" N.O. Bardal	" A.W. Prendergast
" D.A. Golden	Lieut. H.L. White
Lieut J.E. Dunderdale	" J.E. Park
" H.E. Mackechnie	" R.A.H. Campbell
" R.W. Queen-Hughes	" R. Maze
" T.A. Blackwood	" A.S. Black
" L.B. Corrigan	" J.D. McCarthy

- ATTACHED -

Capt. H.A. Bush	Capt. G.M. Billings
" G. Porteous	" U. Laite

- HOSPITAL -

Capt. D.G. Philip - Lt. F.V. Dennis - Lt. W.F. Nugent

- IN SPIRIT -

Lt-Col. J.L.R. Sutcliffe	Major A.B. Gresham
Capt. A.S. Bowman	Capt. L.T. Tarbuth
" E.L. Terry	Lieut C.A. Birkett
Lieut C.D. French	" C.B. Harper
" J.A. David	" R.J. Hooper
" E.L. Mitchell	" W.V. Mitchell
" O.W. McKillop	" H.J. Young

thing than that luxurious tub Mondays and Fridays at 2:00 p.m. I then came back and had a sleep and then visited the men in my company. During the morning I visited all my men in the three hospitals: the Dip., the General, and the Dip. convalescent wards. I have over 40 in the various wards. I gave them a few smokes each and had a chat. That took up nearly two hours. In the afternoon I called on some of the officers of the Royal Rifles, then came back and got all dolled up for our Christmas dinner. I wore khaki shorts and puttees, a shirt with tie (the tie was given to me by one of the Rifle officers. I didn't own one), and a khaki tunic. We sat down about 6:30 and had a can of meat and vegetables each, a

147

roll (bread), Christmas pudding made in our kitchens served with a cinnamon sauce, and tea with milk and sugar. We each had a menu and toast list with all the officers' names, including those that are gone. I will show it to you, it is really a nice one. Lt. Dunderdale made them. We had a short concert after the dinner and then came back to our rooms.

Yesterday we were busy all day getting ready for a big inspection that took place this morning. It is quite a job keeping a wreck of a place like this in any sort of tidy shape, but we got it looking fairly decent. This morning we had an early breakfast and started in all over again getting the lines cleaned up, and about noon (one hour late) two lieutenant generals, a major general, and a flock of colonels and their staffs descended on us. The Japs are great for stage-settings. They had the men playing baseball. Our men played the Royal Rifles and the British troops played football, and down in the church they had a concert on for about an hour and a half. The Japs like to give the impression that we are a great big happy and contented family here, living the life of Riley (the Bs). That finished about 1:00 p.m. so we have been carrying on as usual this afternoon. Every evening we sit around and read or sing songs, with Jack Bailie playing the uke. We have been most fortunate in the weather for the past two months. It will gradually get colder and Feb. and March are really stinkers here. The winds are so cold and blow all the time from the north. We are better clothed than we were last winter, and our huts are gradually being put in shape to keep out the winter weather. There is, of course, no heat of any kind, so one has to keep moving or put on everything they own at night to be comfortable. Here we are, about to start a new year. I wonder what it will hold for us, Sweetheart. I hope it means my homecoming. There couldn't be anything as wonderful as that would be. We try not to think of it too often as we get feeling so darn low, but it is always the foremost thing in our minds just the same. Good-bye for tonight and all my love to you both. I hope Santa was wonderfully good to you both.

Ken & Daddy

Friday, January 1, 1943

Dearest Molly and Harvelyn,

At this moment it is about 10:00 p.m. New Year's Eve at home, 12:30 New Year's Day in Hong Kong. My wishes for you both, good health, peace of mind, and happiness forever, and that is a long time. I hope, Molly, you are at a party having a bang-up time. Our New Year's Eve was celebrated by attending company concerts. Pretty awful, some of them, but gave the boys something to laugh at. We had a cup of cocoa and of course got awfully tight on it. In other words just another evening, only the Japs allowed the lights to stay on until 12:30. It is nice and bright today, but chilly. There is a ball game on, our officers vs. the British and Hong Kong Volunteer officers. I can hear them cheering, the game has just finished, but as to who won I don't know yet. I start the New Year out in the right way: it is my day for a hot bath, so I will be sweet and pure once more. We haven't made any preparations for a special dinner; our rations won't stretch that far. But we will manage all right. For breakfast I had rice and a fried sole. It was good too. Our main meal is at night. The mess waiter just came in collecting our small enamel saucers, so it looks as though we may have pie tonight. We get no news of the outside world these days and it leaves us wondering just how things are progressing—I hope well for us.

Again a Happy New Year to you both and loads of love,

Ken

Tuesday, January 5, 1943

Dearest Harvelyn,

Many, many Happy Birthdays, Sweetheart. This morning just after our parade,

Maj. Bailie, Capt. Norris, Capt. Philip, Capt. Walker and Capt. Prendergast came into my room and I took out your picture, Dearest, and wished you a Happy Birthday, and we all sang Happy Birthday to you, dear Harvelyn. I don't know who started it, but I thought it awfully nice of them to do it. How I wish I could be with you today, Punkle. I hope you will receive a lot of nice birthday presents and that Mummy got you one from me. I am so far away, and so lonely and homesick to see you and Mummy, but I hope it won't be very many more months.

Best love for a very happy birthday and lots of fun and happiness to both you and Mummy,
Daddy

Thursday, January 7, 1943

Dearest Harvelyn,

You are quite a grown-up young lady now and how I wish I could see you and all the presents you received. I wonder what Mummy gave you. I am sure you love it, because I know Mummy would give you something awfully nice. Hello, Molly Dearest. I hope you have recovered from the festive season. Did you have fun? I hope so, Sweetheart.

It has been awfully cold here for the past two days. The temperature is 57 above zero and we are all nearly frozen. The reason is we are used to heat and hot weather now. Nobody in our units is in shape to stand the cold, even if we had the proper clothes. Then we never have a fire of any kind, not even a little bit of blaze, so for the next three months we can count on it being continuously *cold*. I have just finished making a pair of mittens. They are a thing of beauty I can tell you, but they do keep my hands warm. I made them out of a piece of khaki cloth. There isn't any news, dear, but this scrawl is just an excuse to talk to you on paper. Hope there will be something to write about soon.

Best love,
Ken

Friday, January 8, 1943

Hello, Sweetheart,

We were awakened at 6:30 this morning by the bugler blowing the fall-in at the "double." That means in a h—— of a rush—so we tumbled out of bed and put on all the clothes we possessed, because the past three days have been awfully cold, and finally landed on the big parade square. It seems they are changing the commander of this camp, who happens to be Lt. Wadda, the commander we had at North Point camp. He was very decent to us there so I hope he will continue to be the same. He has just returned from Japan, having been away three months. He was in charge of the ship carrying British prisoners to Japan that was torpedoed.* I hope he hasn't acquired too much "culture" since leaving North Point. I went down to the kitchens this morning and split wood for half an hour, got some good exercise and thoroughly warmed up for the first time in days. Jack Bailie is wallowing in a hot tub and I go for mine at 2:00 p.m. Mondays and Fridays are red letter days, when we have our hot swims. I have just made a pot of tea with the electric water heater we manufactured. It works like a charm, so does our toaster. They, along with I don't know how many others, are hard on the fuses, but toast does taste darn good with our meals even though we do have it dry. Ernie has just dropped in and is having a mug of tea. Bye for now.

Love,
Ken

* We found out after the Japs surrendered that this Lt. Wadda was the cause of hundreds of our British men being drowned. He kept them battened down under hatches and they drowned like rats. Any that got out were machine gunned.—*Ed*.

153

Shamshuipo—"roll call"

154

Since Monday of this week our whole camp has been in an uproar. The Japs are taking about 1,600 troops from this camp to Japan—we think—600 Canadians, the rest Imperials, no officers excepting Capt. Reid, our medical officer. They have been kept busy with inoculations, swabs, etc., etc. They will be refitted with clothing in a day or two and probably leave in a week's time. It will, more than likely, mean the breaking up of this camp. I have felt as low as the devil all week long at the thought of the men going. Thirty-eight of my men are on the draft, including Fay. I hate to see him go, he is a cheerful little devil. Our camp has been all upset, and we are getting along on pretty slim meals, as nearly all our cooks are on the draft. We understand there is to be another Red Cross parcel in a few days. Last Tuesday there were about 100 letters arrived from Canada, mostly from Eastern Canada. There must be thousands of them somewhere. How I wish I could get one from you and Harvelyn with some snaps in it. I hope I will have one in the next lot. Owen Hughes got a letter that had been posted in Halifax. Will write more soon, Sweetheart.

Best love for now,
Ken

155

Dearest Molly and Harvelyn,

The camp has settled down after a week's turmoil and general upset. Another draft has left this camp for Japan. They left yesterday at noon, sailing on the *Asama Maru*, one of the Japanese luxury liners. There were 1,200 in all. Of this number, 600 were Canadians, so our battalion is all shot to pieces. The men we have left, excepting the officers, are pretty much all crocks. For the past five days the draft have been isolated. Yes, for just over one week in fact. They have been inoculated four times, swabbed, vaccinated, outfitted with some new clothes, given 10 yen to spend on the boat, and given a bottle of beer at the dock. All the Canadians were given third-class bunks to sleep in and were apparently most thrilled. They were lucky to have such a nice boat to go on; the other drafts were packed in small freighters like sardines and had a pretty awful trip I have heard. What they will do with the rest of us the Lord only knows, but they are sure to stir up something soon. There is a gang of men now cleaning up the lines—and how they need cleaning.

We have had beautiful weather for the past two weeks. I hope it continues for another month. I dread the cold winds that blow continuously through Feb. and part of March. The Col., Harry Hook, Ernie Hodkinson and Jack Norris, as well as some of the other officers, have hot foot and are all feeling pretty miserable. Can't think of anything else to write about now, so cheerio, Sweetheart.

With all my love,
Ken

Wednesday, January 27, 1943

Dearest Molly and Harvelyn,

It has been one week since I last wrote anything. There has been plenty doing in that time. As I have told you, the draft left on the 19th. We have all been moved into different huts, concentrating all the troops on one side of the road and moving all the hospitals into the huts across the street. . . . The Jubilee Bldg. is now empty. A building containing 80 apartments was used as the Dip. hospital. I don't know what they plan to do with it now. We had two days *darned* hard work moving and carrying patients and their beds and effects from the various hospitals to their new location. I thought I was feeling in the pink of condition, but two or three loads made me realize that I am just a softie, so I took it a bit easier the rest of the time and felt like the devil after it was over.

One of my men, L/Cpl. Singleton, died two days ago, the result of general deficiencies caused by lack of food and treatment. A darn fine lad. Has been with me from the start. I have lost quite a few to date and it makes me see red to think all these deaths have been so unnecessary. They wouldn't have happened if we had been allowed the proper food and medical supplies.

We have our hut fairly comfortably fixed up now. I built a dining table yesterday and am quite proud of my effort as it gives us room to sit and eat our meals in comfort. The Portuguese in camp put on a show Sat. night. It really was excellent, and they are putting it on for the third time tonight. I am going to see it again, wish you could come. No, I don't—I wouldn't have you in this damn country for all the gold in the world.

Ken

Saturday, February 6, 1943

Cold and rainy today. Jack Bailie is taking a bath in the corner of the room. Bucky Walker and Bob Philip are bothering the life out of him and passing all kinds of bright remarks. The papers here the last day or two have said the Germans are taking a good trimming in Russia. I hope it is true. I hope they soon get them cleared out of North Africa, then smash Italy. Then we will see the end in sight in another year's time. I have heard on fairly good authority that the International Red Cross man has written Tokyo stating the local Japs have pilfered 30 per cent of the Red Cross parcels brought to the Far East. There were enough for three parcels for us, we have heard. We have had one, delivered on Nov. 29. The balance are in barracks but they won't release them and God knows the men need them so badly. No news, and nothing to write about.

Ken

Friday, February 12, 1943

Nearly a week since I last wrote anything and during that time have been in hospital for two days and feeling sort of rotten the rest of the time. Last Sat. we were given something in our food that put five of our officers in hospital and all the rest, excepting me, to the cleaners. The five of us have had another touch of dysentery and the rest about as bad. Whatever it was played merry hell with our digestions and we are still feeling pretty much washed out. Nearly half of the Canadians are in hospital and 30 are going over to Bowen Road Hospital in Hong Kong today, and believe me they need to go. Our hospitals in the lines are ghastly. The buildings are about the size of the sheep sheds at Brandon Fair

Grounds, only closed in, and just about as warm. All the windows are bricked up or closed in with tin or matting to keep the wind out. There isn't one speck of heat of any kind in the whole camp and just barely enough wood for cooking the meals. It is a damn shame too. There are hundreds of Red Cross parcels in camp and the Japs won't release them for distribution. The diet in hospital for the first day was nil. That suited me OK. I wasn't interested in food at all, but they gave me two copious doses of salt. Very tasty. The second day for breakfast a little ground rice that looked a little like cream-of-wheat: no salt, no sugar, no milk and plenty of lumps. For lunch a little fish soup and some "green horror" boiled greens. At night, a piece of fish about the size of a 50 cent piece and the fishiest fish I have ever tasted. I told them I was all right at the end of the second day and returned to my own little hole in the wall. We—Jack Bailie, Jack Norris, Bob Philip and I—are in a room about half the size of Dad's garage, not any more room than three-quarters the size at best. We have made it fairly comfortable, what with our home-made electric toaster and water boiler. We make toast and tea and warm our room up a bit by leaving the toaster on. We really are all right and, in fact, darn fortunate. Then we have a few rats that gambol about our room at nights. We have a great laugh at Jack Bailie and his electric rat traps. So far it has blown the fuses several times, given us several bad jolts, but I can picture the rats thumbing their noses and having a great laugh. The devils certainly don't go near them, at least not yet. It is nice and bright today and fairly warm. Much nicer than this time last year it seems. Bye for now.

Best love,
Ken

Sunday, March 7, 1943

Haven't written anything since Feb. 12. Have been in hospital with dysentery for 19 days and was sick several days before they admitted me. Just got out last night and feel sort of weak in the knees yet. Friday they sent 60 more to Bowen Road Hospital and brought back 20 that had been up there for some time. Two weeks ago we received our second Red Cross parcel. You have no idea how we appreciate them. The little extras we get seem to taste so good, and the boys cheer up and seem to improve in health right away. We have about 700 Canadians in camp and about half of them in hospital, with more going every day. Everyone is suffering from some form of malnutrition. It takes the form of sores and burning feet, pellagra, Dip. (two new cases last week), heart trouble, and scabs. It is heart-breaking to go into the agony ward where the men are suffering from hot feet. They go days without sleep and just sit and rub their feet and some of them cry with the acute pain. We have had a few go off their heads with it, and all due to lack of proper food. I never thought it possible to see the result of what the wrong kind—or I should say shortage—of food will do. Rice and greens and fish, darn little fish, are what the Japs bring in. The Red Cross have supplied the flour, sugar, and bully beef we get and 2 oz. of meat per day, plus a completely starchy diet is playing hell with the troops.

You will have to excuse the scrawl—I am as blind as a bat from pellagra, my lips feel as though I had a local anaesthetic at the dentist, I can hardly see to read a book and can only stick at it for about half an hour, and am in darn good shape in comparison to the average. Well, that is enough of being glum. The interpreter told the brigadier there were tons of mail in the colony for the troops. It is being censored. If we could only get some mail from home it would make us all feel like a million dollars. We haven't been allowed to write home since last year about 10 months ago, so you couldn't possibly get mail, but, Sweetheart, it isn't because I haven't wanted to write. I have thought so much and dreamed so often of you and Harvelyn. I do hope you are both well and as happy as can be.

Love,
Ken

You know Lord, how one must strive
At Samshuipo to keep alive.
And how there isn't much to eat—
Just rice and greens at Argyle Street.
It's not much, God, when dinner comes
To find it's just Chrysanthemums.

Nor can I stick at any price
Those soft white maggots in my rice.
Nor yet those little hard black weevils,
The lumps of grit and other evils.

I know, Lord, I shouldn't grumble,
And please don't think that I'm not humble
When I most thankfully recall
My luck to be alive at all

But, Lord I think that even you
Would soon get tired of ersatz stew.
So what I really want to say
Is: If we soon don't get away
From Samshuipo and Argyle Street,
Then please, Lord, could we have some meat?

A luscious, fragrant, heaped-up plateful,
And also, Lord, we would be grateful
If you would grant a living boon
And send some Red Cross parcels, soon.

"A Prisoner's Prayer," composed by an unknown Canadian officer.

163

I haven't written anything for 16 days. I came out of the hospital on March 6, Sat. night, and went back in again on Monday with the dysentery (36 days all told) and think this time I am cleared of it. I hope so in any case. If you can read this you are doing more than I can.

Saturday was my red letter day since arriving in this heathen country over 16 months ago. Your letter arrived, Sweetheart. I couldn't help crying, I was so darn glad to hear from you and know you both are all right, even if the news is nearly 11 months old. I only hope the last 11 months have been healthy and happy ones for you both and that your other letters will arrive soon. There are tons of mail downtown somewhere that have been in Hong Kong since last Sept. and never delivered, but we hope now it will start coming through. The pellagra I have has left me so blind I can't see what I am writing but I hope you may be able to make it out if you ever see it. I could tell your writing but couldn't read it and one of the men in the hospital read it to me. I don't think this will be for long, as I am taking everything I can buy to build up the deficiencies in my system that are causing this trouble. So many have it and worse. Otherwise I am as healthy as a trout, now that dysentery is over. I am so glad about Harvelyn's radio and bike. Do you really like the tray? You know how little chance I had to think of Christmas, and besides, it was only October. I had something here ready to send but the scrap starting when it did spoiled every chance so they are all gone with everything else I owned. But remember one thing, my sweetheart. We have at least three Christmases and all other holidays to make up when I get back, and won't I love that. Must stop now, can't see where I am supposed to be writing.

Best love,
Ken

Tuesday, April 6, 1943

A year ago today Col. Sutcliffe died. Yesterday we had the first heavy rain since last fall. The camp was flooded and the rats were drowned out of their nests. The men and a dog killed 30 of them.

[K.]

Wednesday, April 7, 1943

Cold and raining today. We got soaked on our morning parade, which doesn't help at all, owing to the lack of extra clothes to change into. The men are getting

10 yen from the Red Cross today so are quite happy. Unfortunately the canteen is nearly empty excepting for cigs. Every evening after our evening "meal" I do about a mile up and down the road in camp trying to get in shape for—just what! I have asked the compradore to try and get me a reading glass. I can't even make out the headlines in the paper and the days seem awfully long, but I am lucky to be in darn good health and am hungry for all my meals. I wish we could get some real war news. We seem to be lost here without knowing what is going on.

Ken

Easter Sunday, April 25, 1943

Dearest Molly and Harvelyn,

I have been thinking so much of you both lately and particularly today. I went for a mile walk up and down the street in front of our huts before breakfast. Had two eggs for my breakfast that I bought on Tuesday and saved. Have been inoculated for cholera and it is just 10:00 a.m. We were inoculated last week for amoebic dysentery; everyone's arm was sore for two days. I took the work party out to Kai Tak airport last Wednesday to cut grass. The airport is progressing slowly. There has been a tremendous amount of work done by man power, and women as well. The women do the work of men. The Japs have demolished thousands of buildings, an area from Victoria Street in Brandon to the C.P.R. and from Twenty-Fourth St. to as far east as houses are built. They just turned the people out of hundreds of apt. houses.

I can see you both going to church today. I am going at noon and will offer up a prayer for your happiness and well-being. I hope we aren't here for another Easter. I want to go home to *Mama*. We don't get any real news, so everything is so slow and time passes particularly slowly for me since I can't see to read. I can't see what I am trying to write now so you will have to excuse all errors in everything. John Crawford has put my name down on the list to be taken over to Bowen Road to have my eyes tested for glasses. I hope I can get some that will enable me to see and recognize people before I bump into them. Oh! Harvelyn, we have the cutest little kitten. We get lots of pleasure out of it. It climbed up Don Philip's pant-leg the other day and he had to take his pants off to get it out. We are expecting to get a Red Cross parcel on the 29th of April. It is the birthday of His Majesty the Emperor of Japan. Maybe they are saving letters to be distributed that day too. I hope so. We haven't had any for two weeks. Good-bye for now.

With all my love,
Ken and Daddy

Dearest Molly and Harvelyn,

Your letter of May 10 arrived today, also one from Mother, just one year after you wrote it. You have no idea how wonderful it was to receive it, also Mother's. I got Jack Norris to read them to me and I wore my dark glasses so the old tears wouldn't be too evident. This scrawl may not be legible. However, I must try and express my feelings of happiness at hearing from you. I am sorry to hear of your Uncle Jim's death and Harvey Sanderson at Pearl Harbor. Some day we will repay the Japs for that. I am taking shark oil and some powders daily, also getting a shot in the thigh of nicotinic acid for my eyes. It feels like a kick from a frozen boot and really hurts for a little while. This treatment is one of vitamin A and B. The shark oil is vitamin A, the powder B_1, and the kick in the pants is B_2. A week ago today they took me to Bowen Road Hospital and tested my eyes. They can do nothing as far as glasses go, and I must build up the vitamin deficiencies in my body and in that way restore my eye-sight. I hope it will be soon. But I suppose several months will elapse before there will be much change. I haven't been able to read for over two months and can't recognize anyone until I am within four or five feet of them. Am feeling just fine, and weight 157. We got our third Red Cross parcel last week and have appreciated it so much. No sign of parcels [from home] and don't suppose they will ever arrive. We would appreciate smokes so much, the cigs. here are awful. It is very hot now. I am only wearing a fundoshi and you would be surprised how scanty my apparel is. Best love for now to you both and I hope the parcels come along.

Ken

May 21, 1943

Dearest Molly,

How I wish I could be with you today. Birthdays seem to roll around and this, your 21st,* will I hope be a happy one. Every day that passes is one that brings us nearer to each other, and the weeks seem to slip by with a monotonous regularity. Here it is, nearly the middle of 1943, and by this time next year surely there will be some sign of the end. Remember when we sat listening to the radio in Brandon the day war was declared and I said it would be finished in Oct. or Nov. 1943? I had no idea of being in this part of the world, but thought only of the Germans. We get no news but what is printed in the paper and of course it doesn't look very bright for our side. However, we are all optimistic and cheerful; that is

* Mum always kept her age a secret—she was always 21.—*Ed.*

one thing we all are—cheerful. I wish I had some snaps of you and Harvelyn. Your letters have been godsends. Am feeling fine and that means a lot. It has been raining a bit lately and the wet season is past due so I expect we will get plenty of moisture the next few months.

Ken

Tuesday, June 29, 1943

Hello, Sweethearts,

Another year has passed over my head and another birthday has caught up to me. Needless to say, it couldn't be celebrated but I hope the next one we will be all together. Have decided to start a diary so here goes. I can't, of course, put much in it as there is so little to write about and news is very scarce. Am feeling fine and weigh 148 pounds. It is awfully hot these days, around 91 or 92 and that is hot as the weather is so humid. We wear as little as possible and stay out of the sun during the heat of the day. We work a bit in the garden behind our quarters, and it doesn't take much exercise to tire us as the food we get doesn't give us much strength. The letters we have received have been so wonderful and cheer us up no end. I wish we had some news as to how things are going. The reports in the paper here are very encouraging for us.

Ken

Wednesday, July 14, 1943

Wednesday, July 14, 1943

Have just heard we have invaded the Italian Islands. Hope they soon put them to rout. No news. We just live to eat what we can get. Have had lots of rain during the past month.

[K.]

Thursday, August 26, 1943

Haven't written anything for a long time, absolutely nothing to write about. On the 15th of Aug., 500 left our camp for Japan (we think), including 200 Canadians. Then a week ago today we were warned to be ready [to move] in half an hour.

We are at Argyle St. where there are 520 all ranks, in very close quarters, but the change will do us a lot of good. Yesterday we had two air raids and we got a kick

Dear Daddy,

How are you? I hope you are well. We are up at Nana's now. I passed to grade seven this year. So now I am finished.Grosvenor school. I am growing so much you wouldn't know me, I weigh 103 and am now nearly as tall as Mum. Diane and I had a lovely two weeks at the lake. I am 5 feet 3 inches tall. We are enclosing two snap shots, which we hope you like. I love singing now and I may take lessons this year. Well I hope I see you soon.

Much Love and Kisses. Harvelyn

172

out of them. One stick of bombs fell about 300 yards away and kicked up an awful row. Fortunately it was just over the brow of a little hill. They were trying for the shipyards nearby and came close to a hospital. We go out on grass-cutting parties each day and once in every nine days we have to go to the kitchens and peel vegetables. The meals are gosh-awful. Just rice and green horror is issued, along with a very little fish. We spend all we can afford to make things half palatable.

[K.]

Sunday, September 5, 1943

Sometime in the night it started to blow and rain and for the past 10 hours has been going like mad. The typhoon warning is up. It comes in 10 stages and no. 9 is now flying. The first seven stages give distance, direction of wind, and course the storm is following. When it gets to the ninth stage anything can be expected. We hope it will miss us, as our huts are not built to take a real storm. In 1937, they tell us, a typhoon did millions of dollars' damage. The instruments of the observatory registered 163 miles per hour and then blew to pieces. At this moment our hut looks like a swimming pool. We have had several air raids lately and a lot of damage seems to have been done—a big fire where they blew up some oil storage tanks. Our meals are pretty drab these days: rice, greens, bread, and tea, morning, noon and night. They increased our pay ¥30 per month, so we will be able to buy a few extras through the canteen, I hope. Am feeling well; weigh 149 pounds, but not a lot of pep to spare. War news seems a little better according to the paper we get in daily. Wish I were with you today, Sweetheart.

Love,
Ken

1-33/3 (S.A.A.G.)
DEPARTMENT OF NATIONAL DEFENCE
(Army)
Monument National Bldg.
OTTAWA, Canada
December 6, 1943

To the next-of-kin of Canadian
Prisoners of War in the Far East.

A consignment of mail, among which were 979 letters from Canadian Prisoners of War in the Far East, arrived on the *Gripsholm* a few days ago. I realise that many relatives and friends will be greatly disappointed at not receiving a letter at this time, especially in cases where the prisoner is interned at Hong Kong. It has, however, been ascertained that most of the letters have come from prison camps in Japan and only a very few from Hong Kong. The reason for this is that although the Japanese exchange vessel called at Hong Kong to pick up the civilians who were being exchanged, no mail was put on board at that point, apparently because the Japanese authorities insist that all mail from Hong Kong must first be sent to Japan to be censored. This causes great delay. The only mail from Hong Kong in this shipment, therefore, consists of letters sent some time ago from Hong Kong to Japan.

I hope that if you have not received a letter, you will not take this as an indication that there may be something the matter with your dear one who is a prisoner. Lists of casualties now come forward regularly and as you have not been notified in this regard, you have every reason to believe that he is safe, even though he has not been given an opportunity to write to you.

The latest information about food conditions is that the rations are only fairly satisfactory, and it has been learned from civilian internees repatriated from Hong Kong that relief supplies and medicines there were sufficient to last up to the end of October. In this connection, a large consignment of food and medicines for the Far East was shipped on the *Gripsholm* in September last, and the Canadian authorities are doing everything possible to ensure that these are made available at Hong Kong and other points without delay. These supplies are estimated to be sufficient to augment the prisoners' rations and medical supplies furnished by the Japanese for six months.

For your information, the Canadian Government has arranged for a sum of money to be given to each prisoner at Christmas.

Yours sincerely,
F.W. Clarke
Colonel,
Special Asst. to the Adjutant-General.

Monday, February 14, 1944

Hello, Sweethearts,

It has been months since I have written anything. There is so little to say. We have had quite a few air raids by our planes and blackouts during the full moon and generally a pretty boring time. Our rations are not so hot. Rice three times a day with a little fish some days, one and a half ounces per person. The Japs talk a lot about their cultural influence in the countries and islands they have occupied. They dwell a lot on the [Greater] East Asia Co-Prosperity Sphere, but they are damn poor on supplies. A number of times we haven't had wood to cook our meals, and lately it is getting to be a bit thick. We had had some good vegetables and no fuel to cook them with. Yesterday (Sunday) we hadn't any meat at lunch time or at night or this morning (Monday), so we are getting a bit gaunt around the belt line and, until wood comes in, it will carry on. They promise us wood and that is as far as it goes.

Best love,
Ken

Sunday, March 12, 1944

Dearest Molly,

Yesterday was a banner day for me. I received two letters from you, one written Nov. 13, 1942, the other Dec. 13, 1942, just 16 months since you wrote them. I have had two other letters from you. They came about 10 months ago and were both over one year getting here. I know there are simply dozens and dozens on their way, and there are just as many for you as they will allow us to write. I have a feeling, though, that ours don't get very far on their long road home. On March 1, I got a letter from Dad; you haven't any idea how glad I was to receive it.

It was full of news and I nearly had a breakdown when I read about his bag of mallards. How I wish I could just have one good meal of them, in fact a meal when one could have meat at all. Our menu is not what one would call inviting. For instance, the following is what we receive daily: breakfast, rice and ground rice without milk, sugar, salt. That is all. Sometimes we have greens, a bit of the following vegetables: carrot tops, potato tops, spinach, cabbage, sometimes two of the above, never all of them at one time. At noon, usually *rice*. . . . At night we usually have a vegetable stew and rice, sometimes a kedgeree made of rice, fish (boiled or baked) and some sweet potatoes mixed in it. They bring some fish in to the camp each day. It works out at two ounces for each person. This includes heads and innards and what heads and paunches they have, because the fish we get is really nothing. Since we have been in this camp (Argyle St.) they have brought us one tin of bully beef each (12 oz.) and one tin of meat and vegetables. Fortunately we can buy a few things in the canteen, but the prices are now so high we get very little for our money. For instance: cocoa, 70 yen per pound; butter, 18 for 12 oz.; a two pound tin of syrup, 11.40; the same in molasses, 10.50; cigarettes, 50 yen for 10; a small cake of shaving soap, 3.50; a lead pencil, 1.50; a tin of berries a third the size of those at home, 1.55. No bread, can't get flour, so our meals are fairly boring from lack of variety. Jack Bailie got a letter from Eva yesterday also. I loved getting yours so much, and Harvelyn's too. She will look lovely in her new skating outfit and serving at a tea (I hope she said). I will have two women to greet me on my return.

Friday night we had a honey of an air raid. The Yanks came over and blistered some place in the city of Hong Kong or in the harbour. We were all confined to our huts and could only listen in on what took place. They were around for well over half an hour. The Russians seem to be going great guns, but our armies seem to be dead from the heels up. Harry and Ernie are both in hospital, so is Col. Trist. George has been in for two and a half months, Ernie for one and a half months and Harry two weeks. Everyone is pretty thin and there is little or no chance of putting on weight on this diet.

Best love for now,
Ken

Monday, March 13, 1944

A gorgeous day. We have had a wonderful winter, not very much cold weather at all and no rain, only a few days in the past four months. Thank the Lord for that. Living in the huts we live in without any heat at all and a leaky roof makes us appreciate good weather. About two months ago I was in hospital for three weeks nearly, and have felt the cold in my back and legs so much since. . . . About 10 days ago I got chilled and that unpatriotic "Italian" disease, lumbago, has had me in its grip. I am feeling better today, but it is a hell of a job getting out of bed when one has to do so. Most everyone has a touch or more of pellagra. My face and scalp feel as though I had received a very powerful local anaesthetic from a dentist. Also my chest is sort of screwy, but it isn't serious. I am to see the med. officer in the morning and will likely start on a course of shots in the arm. Our canteen comes in tomorrow. Hope it brings some syrup, as I can hardly get the breakfast rice down without something to help it along. How long! How long! will this damn thing last. I hope we will all be able to hang on to ourselves and act like good soldiers should, but it is damn trying at times. I guess I must be still having that indigo feeling that letters from home can't help but leave one with. But how good getting the letters is, especially after 10 months without a single one.

Bye,
Ken

Dearest Molly and Harvelyn,

Am feeling sort of lonely today. We haven't heard any news for a few days so hope that is a good sign. Received a letter from Aunt Maude on Sat. the 18th, just over 16 months since it was written (Dec. 8, 1942). Oh! our mail service is wonderful. Have had six letters since I landed in this heathenish country and I expect you have had less, though I have written each month. One of the boys just came into the hut and said there are some newspapers and letters just come into camp. How I long for a picture of you both. I have the one of you and Harvelyn with the dog in the park and a couple taken in Kingston when you were with Doris. If you could only know the thrill I get when I see your handwriting on a letter. Have been getting more inoculations lately for beriberi.

Ken.

[*March 1944*]

The following appears in today's *Hong Kong News* under Government Order no. 8, date of March 23, 1944, and over the signature of Rensuke Isogai, governor of the captured territory of Hong Kong:

Profit taxes shall be imposed at the following revised rates. Taxes on meals taken by each person at one time:

[Under] ¥5.00—10%   Above ¥50.00—38%
Under ¥10.00—20%   Above ¥100.00—46%
Above ¥10.00—30%   Above ¥500.00—60%

Since the occupation of this territory and the advent of the Greater East Asia Co-Prosperity Sphere, the prices of a few of the food commodities that make life livable in a place like this have advanced as follows, and some of these are now out of sight at our quoted prices here:

Lowest we ever paid	Old (¥)	New (¥)	Lowest we ever paid	Old (¥)	New (¥)
Soya Sauce (2 lbs.)	1.20	6.20	Onions	.60	3.50
Soya Bean Powder	3.50	8.00	Salt	.60	3.10
Soya Beans in sauce	.35	3.10	Jam (local)	.60	3.80
Yellow Beans	.40	3.15	Cigarettes (cheapest)	.10	.40
Sugar	.90	5.65	Matches (small box)	.05	1.30

Syrup (2 lbs.)	.75	11.40	Oranges (each)		13.00
Bully Beef	.65	15.00	Lard (per lb.)	3.00	18.00
Cocoa	2.50	70.00	Peanuts ([per] catty*)		6.00

Two days ago they brought in a supply of rice and it has to last until the end of May. It works out at 13 ounces per day per person. This is before it is washed and all the dirt, stones, etc., are removed. And as rice makes up about 80 per cent of our diet issued by the Japs, I don't think we will put on very much weight. The rest of our diet consists of boiled greens (some not too bad, some not so good) and a few ounces of peanut oil per person each month. So after we make our contribution to the various funds, amounting to about 15 per cent or 10 per cent of our pay, the balance at the previously quoted prices doesn't give us many extras. However, we are still able to laugh at each other and get on without any scraps. Believe me, that is something. Occasionally one of us will blow the lid off some silly thing and then feel foolish for doing it, but that is life. Have prepared a very delectable dish for my lunch. I saved half of my morning rice and have prepared the following (note: try this sometime, mixing very care-

* One catty equals one and one-third pounds.—*Ed.*

fully, then put it all in the "Hoogah" and pull the chain in a hurry): one cup of rice (cooked to a nice gooey mess); four small onions, sliced; one green tomato, chopped up; two cloves of garlic, diced (note 2: you notice I am using all the approved terms used in cookery); salt; pepper; dessert spoon of soya sauce; same of peanut oil; and two dessert spoons of soya bean powder. Put in a tin (with a tight lid) and press down gently and then cover with water (note 3: *Important*. Put pin-hole in lid of tin to let out the steam, otherwise there is a loud explosion and one's efforts have gone to waste). Take to kitchen and put in steam barrel, cross your fingers and pray for favourable results. The efficacy of prayer is also important.

Ken

[*March 1944*]

Have just finished lunch and my goulash was quite a tasty dish. I had Harry, Ernie and Jack try it *first*. They all survived so I took a chance and will now repeat the effort three times each week. . . .

Downtown prices for shoe repairs: rubber heels, ¥10; half soles (leather), ¥45. Fortunately I have two good pairs of shoes because all during the spring, summer and fall I wear wooden clogs. Have worn out three pairs already. Some prices quoted in paper: Pork, ¥28 per catty. . . . Peanut oil, ¥45 per catty. Rice and oil are the principal diet of Chinese in these parts. Well, God help the poor devils.

[K.]

Wednesday, March 29, 1944

A real Christmas day for me. Just received four letters. The first one from you, dated Dec. 8, 1942; one from Marge Fraser, dated Aug. 30, 1942; one from Jess, not dated, but mentions Mother being East and Dad having broken three ribs. I am so sorry to hear of the accident. It takes a lot out of a youngster, and twice as much out of a person Dad's age. He certainly made a wholesale job of it. One letter from Bobby Brown, so I feel very pleased with myself.

[K.]

Thursday, March 30, 1944

Another letter from you, Dearest, dated August 31. I wish you had enclosed some snaps of you two youngsters. You can't imagine how I long to get pictures of you both. There are bags and bags of mail that have been in the colony for over 18 months, and it has just been in the past two months that they have started distributing it. My last letter from you until the present lot arrived was May 10, 1943. It has been sitting a stone's throw from our camp—but just sitting.

[K.]

Thursday, April 6, 1944

We are all just infants once more. The Royal order came out that all lights go out at 9:30, so that means we are all in bed by that time. What a life. This is Good Friday. The baker forgot to bring the hot cross buns so we are having rice instead. It has been so long since I have seen meat that I have almost forgotten what it is like. We have had two days of dull and rainy weather, everything is damp and soggy. Hope it clears up soon so that we can get our clothes dry.

[K.]

We have just been issued with a half pound of peanut oil and a little brown sugar—like the "penuche sugar," if that is how one spells it—pretty low grade too. I have been thinking of you and Harvelyn all day, going to church all dressed up. How I wish I could be with you, there is nothing I could wish for more. Just 27 years ago today I was in the Vimy Ridge show. I didn't expect to get out of that show alive, let alone being on the other side of the world from my wife and daughter. Our Sunday dinner and supper are over. We had rice and boiled greens, that's all. At both meals. How I wished I could be with you, tearing into a meal served as only you can do it, Dear. Oh Lord! How much longer will this last? We do get fed up on this kind of existence. I read as much as my eyes will allow, about one book each week, and then I putter around fixing things. I was on the wood-cutting squad for about six weeks but had to quit it. It was too strenuous. I developed beriberi of the chest and nearly passed out a couple of times so here I am just filling in time once more. I was enjoying it, one hour each day. I am now polishing a brass memorial plaque that I am working on. It is two years since I first started it. Have one side about done and am now working on the back. It is awfully slow work, wearing a rough surface down until it is perfectly smooth, with a piece of brick. When it is done I will engrave it. Have just finished the engraving tool which I made out of a piece of old knife (blade razor). I should have it smooth in a couple of months if I persist.

[K.]

Tuesday, April 11, 1944

Had to visit our dentist this morning. I broke a piece of tooth, and when he took the old filling out the tooth had to come too, as there wasn't enough to put a proper filling in. This damned place ruins one's digestion, eyes and disposition. Every night now we have our lights turned out at 9:30 and as there isn't anything else to do, we go to bed. I am slept out by 6:00 a.m. It is still dark, so have to stay in bed until 7:00 when it gets light enough to see things. Have started thiamine inoculations for my eyes as they are starting to go back again. It is a damn shame when a bit of proper food would correct all the grief we have in camp.

[K.]

Wednesday, April 26, 1944

We have been having about five weeks of fairly wet weather with only a few days of sunshine. All our clothes feel damp and muggy and when the sun comes out everything in the way of a clothesline is full of sheets, blankets, etc., being aired and dried. What a boring and humdrum life this is. Time hangs so heavily on one's shoulders. My eyes won't let me do much reading and I have been doing odd little jobs such as putting up shelves and generally fixing the small space allotted to me in our hut to make everything as compact as possible. Each person has an area about half as large again as our dining room table, so you can imagine that we can't do much wandering without getting into someone else's household.

It looks as though we will be here another year. Everything seems so slow in Europe and we will have to wait until things are cleaned up there before we are relieved here. With our lack of news, the British seem to be doing damn all but some bombing. I wish they would take the lead out of their pants and get really going. We are entertained at night by the rats squeaking and raising hell generally; this camp is crawling with them. Prices are still soaring: a 2 lb. tin of cane syrup, ¥11.40; small onions, ¥3.50 per lb.; bully beef, ¥15.00 for 12 oz.

[K.]

Here we are, back again in Shamshuipo. They say three times and out. We were warned on Wednesday evening to be ready to move at 8:30 a.m. Thursday, so we had plenty of time to get our litter all packed. When one has it all spread out it is a pretty sorry sight comparing it with what we brought with us. Since Monday I have been feeling sort of punk; that is, up to Wednesday a.m. when I developed another bout of dysentery. What a day that was. I felt as though I couldn't lick a postage stamp. However, we got here about 11:00 a.m. and I saw the MO and was in hospital within the half hour. They started feeding me sulpha tablets, and for the next 36 hours I felt very sorry for myself. That, however, is a thing of the past and not interesting anyway. . . . We are segregated and living 50 to a small hut. Our bed space is about 4 feet wide by 7 ½ long with an aisle to come off. We can see the boys in the garden but they are just too far away for me to recognize any of them.

More soon again,
Ken

Sunday, May 14, 1944

Hello, Sweetheart!

One week from today and you will be 21, isn't it? Anyway, you will always be 21 to me. How I wish I could be home to celebrate. What a birthday it would be. I think and dream of you both so much that surely some time soon my dreams must come true. If we could only get some authentic news of what is happening in Europe we would all feel so much better. All we hear is the losses suffered by our navy, army and air force. All the rest seem to get off scot-free. However, there must be the odd casualty every week or two in their ranks, if it is only one of them slipping on a banana peel and knocking his ——— head off. One would never know it is Sunday. They moved my bed in the hospital from one part of the ward to another and are now busily constructing a brick wall. They have just stuck another wire fence up outside. They are building new stoves in the kitchens to cook more *rice* in. Lordy, how fed up I am of it. Nearly 29 months of it and God knows how many more to come. Cheer up, though. We can take it and make them like it.

Ken

Sunday, May 21, 1944

Hello, Sweetheart!

Many happy returns of this date. I have been thinking of you all night and even though it is still before breakfast, I am wondering what you and Harvelyn are doing. I do hope you have bought yourself a nice birthday present from me and that someone is having a swanky party for you. I only wish I could be there to help make it a gala day.

I have been in hospital for 10 days now with dysentery but am feeling more like myself the last three days. They brought me an egg for breakfast. "A real treat," I can tell you. They cost two yen outside. These eggs came from our chicken farm. We get about 12 each day, and they give them to the patients that need them the most, for 30 sen. Cheap, I call it. We are expected to eat them raw. I never could go a raw one but have had two others that I managed to get down by mixing them with my rice and doping it up with soya sauce, etc. I sneaked this one into the sterilizer and cooked it for about 3 minutes, so when our morning rice arrives I hope to enjoy it. How it rained all yesterday and last night. We must have had about five inches of water fall in that time and thundering and lightning all the time. The building we have for a hospital is in the old army canteen, most of the windows are out, and the roof only leaks in two places. My bed, of course, had to

Outside Shamshuipo Camp.

193

be under the worst leak, so they moved me to a dry spot. Since coming back to Shamshuipo they have crowded us into huts like sardines, 50 to a hut. Our bed space is about five feet wide by seven feet long, so we are bound to be in each other's lap and hair all the time. It will be tough when the weather gets hot. There is so little to write about—news, nil—but we are hopeful. Now, Molly o' Mine, keep smiling and your chin up. The doctor has just been to see me and has told me I can go back to the lines this morning, so I must be cured.

Best love, Sweetheart,
Ken

Sunday, July 16, 1944

Hello, Sweetheart!

It has been some time since I last wrote in this old book. However, very little happens to us these days and there seems nothing to put on paper. Jack Bailie has been in hospital for a week with malaria and had one very bad night. Thought he might not pull through; his temperature dropped from 105.6 to 97 in two hours time and his heart went to pieces. He is OK now though. They are keeping him in bed a while yet. I have had two letters since I last made an entry in this book, one from you that was written 22 months ago, the first one you wrote after receiving my letter. You have no idea how wonderful it is to receive mail. Cooped up behind a wire fence for 133 weeks to this date isn't a very exciting experience.

However, we are still alive and receiving two meals a day from the kitchens: rice and boiled pumpkins, beans (Red Cross), and some vegetable tops that are pretty grim when it comes to eating them. Prices are soaring. For instance, soya sauce that used to cost ¥1.20 for 2 lbs. is now ¥8.60. We use a bit to help get the rice down. Soya bean powder, ¥10.80 per pound. Brown sugar, ¥7.80 per lb. Syrup, 2 lbs., ¥19.00. Salt, ¥5.70 per pound. Cigarettes, ¥1.05 per packet of 10. Matches, ¥1.30 for 90 matches. Cigarette papers, 90 sen for 45 papers—as much as nine packets of 10 cigarettes used to cost us. Lard, ¥25, and peanut oil, ¥25. A spool of thread, ¥6.30. And as we get 100 yen per month and contribute 17 or 18 yen to camp funds, we can't buy very much with our money. Luckily we have had two or three issues from the Red Cross of peanut oil, 11 oz. at a time; two of lard (same amount), which we put on our rice to get a little fat into our systems; brown sugar, a half pound; and soya beans, a pound and one-quarter. We grind these up and mix some rice and lard with them and send them to the kitchen to be heated in an oil barrel rigged up as a steamer. It helps a bit in getting the damned rice down. We haven't had meat of any kind issued for over one year; consequently everyone has deficiency diseases of one kind or another. My eyes have been on the bum for the past 20 months. I can see enough to write this but can't read it, so please excuse the many errors you will undoubtedly find. I am glad you can't see me now. I had to have all my hair shaved off on account of pellagra sores, so I look like a peeled onion. I have it shaved every five days. The last time the English padre did it and nicked my head to beat hell. He said this morning he was waiting for me as he had figured out a lot of new designs to carve into my scalp. I sold my fountain pen for 75 yen and a navy rain coat for 100 yen some time ago so I have been able to get extra sugar, syrup, soya sauce, and a few other things. Soap is ¥3.50 a cake. It's about the size of a silver dollar and half an inch thick. I paid ¥10.50 for three cakes, also bought more peanut oil (¥25) and soya bean powder. I have a deal pending for my watch for 500 yen. Hope it goes through. It will keep me supplied for about six months unless prices go out of sight. They allowed us to send two post-cards this month, one to you and one to Dad. I hope they arrive.

It will soon be time to explore and taste the mystery tin I sent to the kitchens to be steamed. It sounds most exciting—like hell—rice, ground beans, six small chopped onions; three cloves of garlic, a spoon of peanut oil, salt, two spoons of sugar and some water added to give it the right amount of moisture. That will be my lunch today as the kitchens cannot cook three meals per day on account of the shortage of wood. We have had rain every day for six weeks and the past few days have been very windy and lots of rain. Must stop now, dearest.

All my love to you and Harvelyn,

Ken

Tuesday, July 18, 1944

We have had some excitement in camp the past two days. Sometime Sunday evening or night, one of the officers in this camp escaped. I think it a selfish thing to do at this stage of the game as he cannot give any information or be of any use in the army on physical grounds. Then everyone in camp is left holding the sack, and a few will really take it on the chin in the way of punishment the Japs hand out. We went on parade as usual at 8:45 Monday morning and came off at about 1:00 p.m., no breakfast at all and just sat out there and waited. It no doubt takes lots of guts to do what that chap did. Nobody knew he was going or a thing about it until he couldn't be found for roll call. It is the absolute truth that not one person had any idea he was escaping, but the Japs don't seem to believe what they are told. They took four officers out for questioning, and they haven't been brought back. Their gendarmes are pretty bad medicine.

Speaking of vermin, I took my bed out this morning and gave it a complete cleaning. It seemed there were at least one million bed bugs in it and it is less than a week since I did it, besides going over it casually daily. These old buildings we live in are simply crawling with them. They drop from the roof at night.

It has been very warm today, over 90 degrees, and the first day without rain for about six weeks. Our meals are all screwy these days, with no wood to cook more than two meals a day, and sometimes tea only once a day. Today they were burning grass and all sorts of dirt and trash to get our supper, and we don't know whether we will have breakfast or not. Some life. However, we are all very streamlined in our undershorts, which comprise daily attire excepting when on parade. Our cooking staff has just told us we will get rice in the morning, but nothing more until wood comes in. Some life. Hurrah, tea has just come up, one granite mug full.

[K.]

Tuesday, July 25, 1944

We have had more or less excitement the past week. First, one of the officers escaped, and we have been collecting the fruits of his departure. Ever so many have been slapped and punched, kicked and hit with rifle butts, and generally bashed about. Then on Saturday it started to blow and we had a new typhoon. The wind reached a velocity of over 100 miles per hour—so said the old timers here—and it played merry hell with our huts. We have very few windows in the huts and every other window is filled with tin or scraps of plaster board or whatever can be found to keep out the rain. Well, these soon gave way, and it was as black as the inside of a cat, with torrents of rain. Well, we had no sleep to speak of and had a meal at 10:30 a.m. and the next at 8:30 p.m. that night. We have had most irregular meal hours for the past few weeks. They won't supply us with the necessary wood for cooking so we can only have two meals per day—if one calls boiled rice with some bran (the kind our farmers feed their stock) mixed in it, and boiled pumpkins and vegetable tops [a meal]. We eat a lot of garlic to give the rice some taste, and everything else, such as syrup, brown sugar, salt, pepper, and soya sauce, we have to buy at the canteen. So you can see they supply damned little in the way of food. Consequently, everyone has some deficiency disease or several diseases.

Ken

Hello, Sweetheart,

    I wonder where you are today. I hope at the lake where it is cool or planning on a nice holiday. I do hope you have been wise and taken a decent one each year, because you need it, and both you and Harvelyn should get away from the city for a while and have as good a time as possible. Two weeks ago tonight, as I mentioned before, one of the officers escaped. I hope he is safe. No one knew a thing about his going, he certainly kept it to himself, but he left a hornet's nest behind. They had a search for him and kept us on parade from 9:00 a.m. until noon without breakfast, and have instituted a lot of extra counts of the huts at night. Yesterday they kept us on parade again until past noon and without breakfast. When one goes from 5:00 p.m. until one o'clock the next afternoon without eating anything, it seems a long time between meals, especially when one only gets rice twice each day and sometimes boiled beans and vegetables once a day. To punish us, who hadn't anything to do with the escape, or knew anything about it, they have stopped our canteen coming in. Believe me, that makes it tough. We are out of cigarettes, syrup, sugar, soya sauce, and everything that helps one to get the rice down. However, we can take it. Yesterday the reason for being kept on parade was that they searched all our effects, and what a mess they left them in, all over the floor and one grand tangle. We haven't had a paper for over two weeks, so haven't any news, but one would think the Japs would by this time know they cannot possibly win this scrap and start being half decent.

I don't know what a state we would be in if it were not for the Red Cross supplies that are sent in occasionally. We don't get much but it does give us a little more to eat. I never thought I could live so long concentrating on nothing but food; everyone is the same. How I wish we could get some news of what is going on in Europe. I feel sure that in two months time the end will be in sight. There is nothing to write about, but my thoughts are always with you both. I have had so many vivid dreams of you lately and of the good times we were having and the meals! Well, when it comes to food I always wake up just as we sit down to one of your superb dinners and it is heart-breaking, I can tell you. It is over 90 today and has been for several days. Our garb here consists of a light pair of undershorts and a smile.

Best love to you both,
Ken

Sunday, August 6, 1944

Hello, Sweetheart,

Harry, Ernie and I have just finished our rice and have been talking about the things we like most to eat. I have just been saying I wish I could just sit at our dinner table with you and Harvelyn and have one of our Sunday dinners—it would just be heaven. Our two meals a day still continue and our hosts brought in a month's supply of rice, short in weight as things usually are, with promises of making up the weight later. Which they never do. We will have a lot of rice and other things should they ever make up back weights suddenly.

Thursday night we had an air raid. They blasted what seemed to be part of the docks. We could feel the blasts over three miles away, so they must have shaken up something down on the water front. It has been raining like the devil for the past two days. We can see the water cascading down the little valleys in the hills. I wish I had some of your maple cream cake and some coffee today, also some cigarettes. We have had the canteen stopped because that chap escaped, so we are getting it in the neck. It makes meal time rather a grim period in a very drab day to look forward to. I hope we are all together this time next year.

All my love.

[K.]

At Shamshuipo—"a talk in a hut."

Hello, Sweetheart,

This is the fourth Tuesday since we have had the canteen stopped on us. It would seem that the whole camp is being punished because of the escape of that officer. It means nobody has smokes and believe me that is tough. We can barely exist on a rice and boiled greens diet, but the lack of smokes makes one ravenously hungry, and only two slim meals per day to go on. Last Wednesday, the Red Cross man was in. He went through the kitchens at noon and asked to see the rice cooking. The messing officer said we didn't get a noon meal, only two a day. He saw a new oven that had just been built and said, "Will you get bread?" and was told we had our last bread seven months ago. Our hosts didn't seem to like it. He then went into one of the huts and one of the officers spoke up in French and English, saying we weren't getting enough to eat and were starving. He was hustled out and locked up in a store room, and the visitors marched off to camp HQ. Then one of the Jap sergeants came back and took a stick and beat this chap over the head into unconsciousness and then kicked him several times. When he came to, they hustled him out of camp and we haven't seen him since. Quite a few have disappeared, never to return. God only knows where they end up.

[K.]

Sunday, August 27, 1944

What a day we are having: Red Cross parcels and meat for our supper. Last week we had brought into us by the Japs a number of pheasants and partridge. It made a marvellous stew. For tonight we are having a stew with over 200 birds in it and we should be really bulging when we finish. These birds are the first we ever had, excepting a few ducks and hens from our own chicken farm; the first in so many months, I have forgotten how long. Today we have been issued with four Red Cross parcels. Such a difference. There are 15 packets in each parcel. You can't imagine what [it's like] getting four pounds of butter, four pounds of milk powder, four tins of marmalade or jam; biscuits, cheese, chocolate, prunes, raisins, corned meat and a sort of ham loaf; salmon and sardines, tea, coffee, sugar, salt and pepper. We have been living on such short rations for so long. I expect a lot will be sick by tomorrow. However, it will be worth it. The Lord only knows how long they have been on the way. Some of the things are in remarkably good shape, though. I am opening all my parcels to see if things are all right.

More later,
Ken

Dearest Molly and Harvelyn,

   Since Sunday noon it seems we have done nothing but eat. We have a snack between meals and some have a snack between snacks. We had a few with upset stomachs, but no wonder. After two years and eight months of a starvation diet where everyone here has been either periodically or continuously ill from deficiency diseases, to get four and a half Red Cross boxes handed to you at one time, full (each one) with what at home is everyday food but to us absolute treats— well, it is a wonder all of us haven't been a bit ill from over-eating. I never thought hardtack biscuits, powdered milk, butter, cheese, marmalade and bully beef could be a royal banquet, but believe me they are. Oh yes, coffee. The kitchen made us coffee yesterday. I could have drunk a gallon instead of half-a-mug full. It is wonderful to walk about our wire mouse-trap and see everyone with a smile on their faces, and a new light in their eyes and a lilt of laughter in their voices. It is surprising how many different kinds of meat, pies and puddings have been concocted from the contents of the parcels. We hear some wonderful and weird rumours every day but we have become hardened to the snares of optimism. Yesterday we received a Christmas card from W.L. Mackenzie King. There must be tons of mail and parcels and millions of cigarettes. We haven't seen or heard of a parcel from home or cigarettes. God knows where they are piled up, spoiling, or who has used them. However, everyone has offered a silent prayer to the Canadian Red Cross Society. We are a few Canadian officers among many British officers and naval officers. Everyone I have talked to has mentioned what a wonderful society our Canadian branch is. That is quite true, but had these parcels come from England, Australia and South Africa, we would all have felt the same.

Ken

Monday, September 4, 1944

In the paper yesterday, the fighting in France and Belgium seems to be over the ground fought for during the last war. We are getting to be so full of optimism that rumours are really running rife. My bet is Germany will be out of it by Sept. 27. A wonderful day in history—for me. And I don't think it will be very much after the Germans quit that our hosts here will be looking for a way out. Some fantastic way to try and save their face—if possible, at the expense of everyone

All Canada joins

in

Warmest Christmas Greetings

and good wishes to you

M. L. Mackenzie King.

1943

Prime Minister

else, including Germany and the rest of their allies. For the past week we have had air raid alarms with planes coming over about 10:15 p.m. For a few nights the Japs put up a barrage, using tracer shells. We could see the shells going up, they looked just like rockets. They didn't hit anything, though. I wish you could know, at this minute, how we appreciate the Red Cross parcels. I have milk and butter at every meal (a little). I want it to last as long as possible. We were so long without anything and our systems were not far from the point where most of us would have started to break up. I will have to start soon taking some exercise or my old paunch, which by the way was one big depression rather than a bulge, will start to come back too quickly. This morning I made a rice pudding and sent it to the cook-house to be put in the steamer. How does this sound for a recipe: three-quarter syrup tin of rice, a little butter, a good handful of raisins, five spoons of syrup, a little salt, and a quarter cup of milk. Don't let *Good Housekeeping* know about this or they will be hounding me for more particulars and there aren't any.

The Japs have brought in during the past few days a lot of Red Cross medical supplies, which we most urgently needed. We should see a lot of the boys out of the hospital during the next month. You will no doubt have some fun trying to make out what I am writing as I can't see to read what I am putting down, and no doubt you will find many misspelled words, etc. However, we shouldn't worry, things are coming our way now.

Ken

Thursday, September 14, 1944

Hello, Sweetheart,

I hope you aren't having it as hot at home as we are here. For the past 10 days it has been pretty awful. Today the thermometer hit 98.5 and the humidity is awful. We go around in our scanties or less and are simply stewing in our own juices, and it lasts nearly all night too. Everyone nearly sleeps in the raw under their mosquito nets or tries to sleep. We are all enjoying a nice dose of prickly heat. Ernie is simply covered from head to foot. We have just been informed there is to be no supper for us. No wood for fires. Lordy, these little brown Bs get one's goat. They are just about as reliable as quicksand. If it weren't for the Red Cross, this camp would be really in a serious condition. A real tragedy has happened to me. One of my cans of Red Cross milk has disappeared and believe me, that is serious.

I will have to stop. The paper is getting so wet it tears, but not with tears.

Best love,
Ken

Hello, Sweetheart,

Just one thousand days ago at this hour, 5:00 p.m., we were taken prisoner. Lordy, how long one thousand days can be, and how much they can mean in one's life. The paper just came in and says our troops are within 20 miles of Cologne. Germany surely won't hold out much longer as she hates fighting in her own country. However, I think they are going to be made to like it this time. We have had our Red Cross parcels now nearly one month and they are beginning to look the worse for hard usage, but how much better we all look and feel. I have gained about 15 pounds. One month ago I weighed 132. I now weigh about 147 and am still 30 pounds below what I have weighed for the past 15 years. Our heat wave has broken at last. We have had three beautifully cool days, and today it has rained all day long. We haven't had light of any kind in our huts for over one month. It gets dark at 7:30 p.m. and we sit about like a bunch of moles, feeling our way through the dark whenever we want to make a move or go anywhere. Must go now. Supper is being served.

Best love, Dearest,
Ken

Wednesday, September 27, 1944

Dearest Molly,

Twenty-two years ago today, the sweetest and most beautiful girl in all the world did me the great honour of marrying me. During the twenty-two years there have been some lean years and some a little less lean, but one thing that has never changed, Sweetheart, is my love for you. How I wish I could be home to celebrate it with you and Harvelyn—but maybe this Christmas may bring much happiness for us all. However, the news seems so encouraging these days and I am sure when Germany folds up, this end of the world will do likewise very shortly after. I hope, Molly, that today will be such a happy one

FROM
K.G. BAIRD.
P.O.W. 4446

PRISONER OF WAR·CAMP
HONG KONG

DEAREST MAYHARVELYN—   OCT. 8./44
ARE YOU BOTH WELL? AM
FEELING JUST GREAT. RED CROSS PARCELS (4)
WONDERFUL. GAINED TWENTY. NOW ONE FOUR
SEVEN. OUR TWENTY SECOND ANNIVERSARY
JUST PAST. ALL HAPPINESS DEAREST.

      HOW·ARE EVERYONE,

MY LOVE TO ALL. PLAN ON NICE
HOLIDAY NEXT SUMMER. KEEP CHEERFUL,
CHIN UP, USUAL SMILE. BEST LOVE
      KEN.

213

for you. If I had a cigarette I would light it and say, "Here's to ourselves," but I say it anyway.

All my love,
Ken

Sunday, October 22, 1944

Dearest Molly and Harvelyn,

It has been over three weeks since I have written anything and we have had a good few air alarms, with only the occasional boom at night when some distant part of the island of Hong Kong or a ship had a load dumped at them. But last Monday, the Yanks came over in force, about 30 bombers. It was a honey of a raid, and the noise was "noisy." The Jap guns firing at the planes sprayed our camp with falling bullets and shrapnel from the bursting shells. In the next two huts to ours one man in each was wounded, one quite badly. His legs were cut up and the bone in one shattered. We have had varying reports about the other camp, where at least 10 and one officer were wounded. The Japs tried to suggest it was from our planes, but they weren't coming from the direction our planes were travelling and then some of the nosecaps from shells picked up were foreign make. How I wish I could be home for dinner today. I am so darned hungry for something but the eternal rice—one gets filled up but still feels hungry. Am going to eat a little rice now (11:00 a.m.) and then at noon more rice. Ye Gods!

Ken

Wednesday, October 25, 1944

Dearest Molly,

Three years ago today we said good-bye to each other at the C.P.R. How long it has been, dear. I know it has been so hard on you, as I am sure my letters aren't getting home. I have written every time they have allowed us to, and you should have at least 20 letters not counting another 10 that could be on the way that I have written. On Monday last, the 23rd, I received your letter written on Jan. 25, 1943, one year and nine months ago. I am sure there are dozens of letters at the Jap headquarters here for everyone here, but they are so slow in delivering them. Your last letter I received three months ago was written Aug. 30, 1942 so you can see they have no system of delivery.

Our Red Cross boxes have all been used up and since they were finished we have been losing weight every week. The past three weeks I have dropped 10 pounds. Today is Jean Hook's birthday, so Harry donated a can of bully beef and we kicked in with a little to make a meat pie. It was darn good too, as we have nothing but rice twice a day, with a little ground beans to make a sort of porridge in the morning, and a few boiled greens at night. For the past two weeks they have been saving some of our rice daily and making a sort of bread with ground beans in it. If eaten hot, one can get it down without too much effort. Tomorrow I am fixing my window against the cold winter winds. I have a piece of corrugated tin and some plaster board to work with. Good-bye for now.

All my love,
Ken

Sunday, November 19, 1944

Dearest Molly and Harvelyn,

If what I have just finished can be called lunch, well, I've had it! Rice, a small teaspoonful of peanut oil, and two cloves of garlic. Does it sound like anything but an insult to one's stomach to you? Meals are, and have been, since our Red Cross parcels ran out, a fairly grim way of keeping the old bones from rattling.

Here it is getting on to three years of this life since we were taken prisoner.

Harry, Ernie, Jack Bailie, and I each saved a tin of bully beef from our parcels and on the 16th we celebrated. It was three years ago that we landed in this heathen country. We weren't celebrating because we came here and have been here three years, but for the fact that we are still alive. We have two tins left for Christmas Day. Prices have soared so high we can't buy hardly anything at all. Table salt is about ¥12.50 per pound, so I buy rock salt, dissolve it in water, filter it to get the dirt out of it and use the brine to season the rice with. It is darn poor stuff at that.

We are holding a handicraft show here on the 30th of Nov. to raise money for the widows and children at Fort Stanley. Each month we contribute about 15 per cent of our pay for this and other camp funds. I have been working on a brass plate that I found in North Point camp two and half years ago, and have been at it ever since. I am showing it at the "Fair." I have been months polishing the bumps and hollows out of it with a piece of brick. Then I had to find steel and make engraving tools and then started work. I got Geoff Bird, an artist, to draw various things in pencil on it and have just finished engraving it yesterday. Darned crude work, I know, but it helped me to fill in many weeks that were darned tough to get over in the past two years since my eyesight has been so bad. I can see things at a distance but not up close, hence the gosh-awful scrawl in this book. I can't read what I write so will just have to try and go through with the proper motions.

We have air raid alarms several nights each week and one night, I think it was Thursday, a plane came over and dropped a load of bombs that made an awful roar. It was a long way off, but something surely got one good smashing up.

We get about 10 packs of cigarettes per month and they don't go very far. If one had reasonable meals it wouldn't be quite so bad. Last Wednesday we all had the Schick test.*

[K.]

Thursday, December 7, 1944

Dearest Molly and Harvelyn,

Three years tomorrow the scrap started, and what a long time it has been. Just at present it is awfully cold. I can hardly hold the pencil to scribble. The nights have been pretty awful. The thermometer goes down into the 40s and when we have a strong wind to rub it in, it gets a bit tiresome. If we had something to eat to put a little fat on the old ribs it mightn't be so bad, and then there isn't any place in camp where one can get warmed thoroughly by a fire. They just don't exist, excepting in the kitchen, and one isn't allowed there or the whole camp would

* The Schick test is a skin test designed to detect diphtheria.—*Ed.*

rush in. I have just finished stuffing a rice-sack bed tick with hay and hope to be a little more comfortable tonight. Yesterday I put weather strips on the door, which is right beside my bed, and stuccoed all the cracks up with mud. Had a regular picnic making mud pies, but it all improved the old shack. Our door faces north, and the wind, they tell me, comes from the Gobi desert, and is really mean.

Last Thursday we had a fair and all sorts of sideshows—pretty corny ones—going full blast. They had a handicraft display, and the work turned out was really marvellous. There are some darn good artists in camp and their work was wonderful. We all had things on display. The Japanese turned out and were surely impressed with what they saw, particularly when one has to manufacture all tools to work with. I hope tomorrow the Yanks will return some of the presents we received three years ago with interest. Well I must move about for a while and stir up the old circulation.

Best love,
Ken

P.S. Oh! I forgot to tell you that in lotteries, sideshows, games and sales of articles they made 2,900 yen for the widows and nurses at [Fort] Stanley. . . . Darn good. In fact, damn good.

Friday, December 8, 1944

Wow! Rescript day came in with a bang. Three years ago at 8:00 a.m. the Japs bombed us, with about 20 planes. This morning about 40 of ours came over and plastered Hong Kong and Kowloon, and machine-gunned the A.A. guns. It was a right merry party. Then at 4:00 this afternoon they came back again, only a few this time, but they seemed to blast the dock areas. I was out in the garden when the bombing started. We had to hustle back to our huts, but on the way I saw our planes diving and heard the roar of the bombs; quite exciting, the more the merrier.

Bye-bye,
Ken

Tuesday, December 12, 1944

In two weeks Xmas will be all over. I am afraid my Xmas shopping will just have to wait for another year. This morning we had one big pig and five little pigs sent in to us by the camp on the other side of the wire. We all dug down and sent money to them last week to buy a few cigarettes for the boys, so they sent us a few pigs. The large one weighs about 200 lbs. and the little ones about 10 lbs.

each, so we should have a slight flavour of pork in our Xmas stew. Pork per pound as shown in the paper is ¥97.30 per 1 ⅓ pounds; egg powder, ¥40; brown sugar, ¥25; dried beans, ¥32.30 per lb.; and dried peas, ¥33.00 per lb.; so there isn't one darn thing one can buy with our pay. The local paper just prints a lot of tripe. We have only had a little news of the European front in the past three weeks, so we don't know a thing about Europe and not much about out here.

Ken

Friday, December 22, 1944

Dearest Molly and Harvelyn,

Today has been a gala day. I have just had a fried egg, fried tomato, and bean and rice bread. About a week ago I made a little charcoal stove out of a tin can, knowing we were to receive an egg when our turn came from the draw we made for turns to receive an egg. From our chicken farm we get about 30 eggs a day, and as we have 470 people in this camp we should get one about every 20 days if the hens and ducks keep working. I received a ½ lb. of tomatoes from our garden so I fried two of them, and believe me they were good. I could have repeated the process at least six times without stopping, as a diet of rice and green beans becomes most uninteresting and tasteless. Col. Tokunaga and the Red Cross representative visited the camp. The Red Cross rep wasn't allowed to speak to anyone or anyone in camp to him, and never has been allowed. At the time he was in, there wasn't one bit of wood to cook our evening meal, so until 5:00 p.m. a little came, so we are having rice and greens two hours late. We are supposed to have a Christmas parcel. I hope it will be a Red Cross box, they are so wonderful. Our Christmas menu is as follows. Rice and bean porridge for breakfast. For lunch, pork kedgeree: boiled rice with bits of fried pork in it. Dinner: pork stew and rice with bread (rice and bean). We bought a pig and five little ones three weeks ago. I have already mentioned it before. They cost 1,500 yen. Pork per pound is selling down in the town, so the paper says, at 116 yen per catty. . . . Sugar now is over 30 yen per pound, and cigarettes 5 or 6 yen per packet of 10. We get 90 cigarettes per month at 65 sen per packet.

We have had for the first 18 days the most damnable weather. Lordy, it has been cold, windy and wet, but the last four days have been bright and much warmer. We have had one or two air raids per day for the past four days. We are so glad to see them and hope they keep it up. There are some real crumps when the bombs go off and, I am sure, quite some damage done. I hope our boxes arrive tomorrow or Sunday. Will write again soon. And listen, Sweethearts, I hope you both have a wonderfully happy and merry Christmas and that the new year will enable us to count the weeks until we are together again. All my love to you both and I hope Santa fills your stockings with everything you would like, including joy and happiness.

Ken

Tuesday, December 26, 1944

Hello, Sweetheart,

Last night was a long and lonely night. I pictured all of you together having one of your or Mother's Xmas dinners, and my mouth watered to join in. Our Christmas dinner was boiled rice with a little bit of fried pork cut up in little pieces, and went by the name of "Fried Pork Kedgeree." Our supper was a stew: potato stew with a little pork flavouring. How I could have tied into about half a pumpkin pie for dessert. And an hour or two after the load of rice we ate had digested, we could have done justice to a real meal.

Yesterday we had four air alarms but no planes. Today we have had three and no planes. They seem to be pretty jittery, because when our planes come, there usually is a bit of hell scattered about. Have had one of my headaches today, couldn't eat any supper, but am feeling not too bad now so will be darned empty by morning. I hope Santa was good to you. I found a hole in my sock. Darned lucky they didn't both have holes.

Best love,
Ken

Wednesday, December 27, 1944

Prices in paper today are as follows: pork, ¥150 per catty (1 ⅓ lb.); beef, ¥90; brown sugar, ¥41 per pound; rock salt, ¥14, the dirtiest and cheapest grade possible for one to conceive. Our pay now per month wouldn't buy 2 ½ lbs. of very cheap and dirty brown sugar. The paper we get daily says the Germans are giving our troops merry hell and the American losses are 10 divisions in about 10 days. I hope it is being grossly exaggerated. Am feeling better today. My eyes give me a lot of trouble, but one can't get glasses that suit. The doctors here haven't any equipment for really prescribing for one's eyes and they can only make a guess to what will suit. Some have paid well over 100 yen (in advance) and then not been able to read or see with them, so I will just have to wait until I get home. Last night I dreamed of you both. You were all so happy and cheery, and trying to tell me so many things that I wakened up and was darn mad at doing so. We had an inspection by some Jap Lt. General. Stood on parade for one and a half hours, and they went past about a quarter of us and buzzed off.

[K.]

Tuesday, January 2, 1945

The new year has come and gone and it was just another day in this hole. We were all wondering where you all went and what sort of a party you were on. I hope a really gay one, and that you enjoyed every minute of it. On Friday next, Harvelyn will celebrate her 14th birthday. How I wish I could be home to see her party. I wouldn't cramp their style, but just to have a short look-see and let them carry on. Our New Year's noon meal was rice, with a little fried fish mixed up in it, and at night rice and veg. stew, the usual old standby.

Sunday's paper said a ship will be leaving Tokyo for points south with American Red Cross supplies and parcels. They have mentioned the American part so much that we are wondering whether we are to be included in the lot that receive them. Today's paper is a scream, the editorial wishing everyone good luck and cheer, etc., for 1945 was a masterpiece of gloom and doubt. Taxes here are really fantastic. Rice per 1 ⅓ pounds (or one catty) costs 29 yen; sugar, somewhere around ¥50 per lb.; pork, ¥150 per catty; onions, ¥50; a tin of syrup, the ones you used to get for Harvelyn, ¥75; cigarettes, ¥5 for 10. . . . Here are rates copied from the *Hong Kong News*, date of Jan. 1, 1945.

Telephone deposit: ¥1,400, plus installation charge of ¥1,400, plus new desk phone: ¥210. Annual telephone charges for Central, Western . . . and Kowloon districts: ¥1,680. Additional charges. Phone extension: ¥504. Cost of insertion of name in telephone book: ¥140. Change of name: ¥140. Removal charge, from one place to another: ¥70; from one part of the house to another part: ¥210. From one house to another house: ¥1,050. Temporary removal: ¥70. And they pay us ¥100 per month, and expect us to buy enough to exist on besides the rice, oil and vegetables they bring in.

Thus the Greater East Asian Co-Prosperity Sphere progresses towards its doom. This year will, I hope, bring war to an end early enough for us to be together during Harvelyn's summer vacation. I am surely counting on it.

Best love,
Ken

Happy Birthday, Harvelyn dear. I wish I could be home to give you the birthday bumps*, along with a big hug and kiss, not to mention a present too. I hope, Sweetheart, you will always be as happy and carefree as you are today. I hope this wish comes true for you. Today we had a small bit of porridge for breakfast, and nothing at noon. Some of us save a little rice from our last night's meal so we had a bit of lunch. There is no wood to cook things with. The Japs are still celebrating New Year's. Nice and cosy here. I hear we will have a bit of supper tonight, but we can take it OK.

Ken

Tuesday, January 9, 1945

Hello, Sweethearts,

I suppose it is as cold as can be at home but I know it isn't bothering you as much as today is bothering us. Everyone is shivering, so we all go out for a brisk

* Where the birthday girl was suspended, held by hands and feet, and "bum-bumped" to the floor.—*Ed*.

walk about camp and get warmed up, and then come back and shiver some more. Yesterday was warm and I had a hot sponge bath. Got a pail of water from the kitchen and went to it. The cold showers only seem to freeze one up solid and I never feel as though I had had a bath. Am going to have a real feed this evening. We all got an egg yesterday, and today we got "cake." You wouldn't have it in your house but it tastes darn good here, so I am going to fry some tomatoes (from our garden) and my egg and have my "cake" with our evening tea, which comes up about seven bells. These darned English have tea at the wrong time: morning at 7:00 a.m., at noon usually before our meal or too late for it, and then about an hour after our evening meal. I have built a little charcoal stove and have collected the charcoal from the kitchen so will build the fire after our parade. Believe me, I can hardly wait.

Ken

Tuesday, January 16, 1945

Dearest Molly and Harvelyn,

Sunday was a red letter day for me. I received a letter from each of you, written Feb. 13, 1944. My first letters for months from you, Sweethearts, so you can just imagine how thrilled I was and still am. They arrived 11 months and one day after they were written. My last letter from you, Molly, was dated Oct. 1942 and I received it while I was in hospital, last May 1944. I know I will never know our daughter when I see her, I am sure. I am so thrilled to think you took part in the Winter Ice Carnival, Harvelyn. There will be so much the both of you will have to tell me. I will be so far behind the times that old Rip Van Winkle won't have anything on me. I am so glad you both received a letter from me. I write every month and have wondered if they ever arrived. Yesterday, the 15th of January, and today the 16th, our air force have been bombing this place for fair. Yesterday they were at it for over two hours and did, I am sure, considerable damage to the shipping in the harbour and the Jap ports and gun positions both on the island of Hong Kong and the mainland. Then at 8:30 a.m. today, our planes started and kept it up consistently until noon. Lordy, how they poured the bombs down. Our hut shook and trembled and the windows rattled, shrapnel hit the huts around us. A pompom shell hit and exploded just outside our hut and broke two windows. Several of the boys were wounded, but not very seriously I understand. We have been kept in all day so far. Oh! The all-clear has just gone so *must* go.

Lots of love to you both,
Ken

Tuesday, January 23, 1945

Last Sunday we had an air raid that lasted a matter of less than one minute, but what a raid! There were between 30 and 40 bombers (heavy) that flew over Hong Kong at about 30,000 feet and all unloosed their load at once and laid a carpet of bombs that, judging from its direction, must have flattened out dozens and dozens of city blocks. It appeared to be around the part of the city where there are two large barracks and all the buildings [are] occupied by the Japanese. The roar lasted a full minute and shook our huts and rattled our windows—and we are about four miles away. This raid, together with the two on the 15th and 16th, must have taken an awful toll. The one on the 16th was continuous for over eight hours. Things really bounced around our huts, with splinters of shells and bullets visiting us occasionally. There were three wounded at our camp. Hardly a day passes without the air raid signal going. It really is interesting and we get an awful kick out of it, and are hoping for bigger and better ones very soon.

[K.]

Hello, Sweethearts,

I suppose it is colder than cold at home now, but it isn't any more uncomfortable than here. For the past two weeks it has been miserable weather, cold, wet and windy, and the barns we live in are graced by the name of barracks. One's hands are like icicles all the time. One's feet also. Conditions are at their lowest ebb now, and what the people outside are doing I can't imagine. We only get rice and a few boiled greens now. We did get a little fish three times a week, a piece not larger than this square [letter shows a block 1.5 inches square]. We have rice porridge with bran in it for breakfast, some rice for lunch, and rice and greens, boiled, at night. There isn't a meal we finish that doesn't leave us ready to go after a meal of any kind and do justice to it.

Last night when we were eating our evening meal, my name was called out and Harvelyn's letter arrived, dated Jan. 11, 1944. You haven't any idea, dear, how glad I was to get it, and the kiss with your Mother's lipstick—or was it your own?—gave me a wonderful kick. The boys all thought it an excellent way to send one through the censors. Why I haven't received some snaps, I can't understand. I long so for pictures of you both. My fingers are numb as my writing must indicate, so good-bye for now.

Best love,
Ken

[*Date unknown*]
Some data given me by Lt. Buchanan, R.N.R., that he has made note of since we have been prisoners of war:

<u>Regiments and Units in Shamshuipo and Argyle Camps</u>

2nd Batt. Royal Scots . . . . .Lt. Col. White

 1st   "   Middlesex . . . . .Lt. Col. Stewart

 1st   "   The Winnipeg Grenadiers . . .A/Lt. Col. Trist; Col. Sutcliffe (dead)

 1st   "   Royal Rifles of Canada . . . . .Lt. Col. Price

 5/7   "   Rajputs . . . . .Lt. Col. Rawlinson

2/14   "   Rajputs . . . . .Lt. Col. Grey

5th A.A. R.A. . . . . .Lt. Col. Field

965—Coast Defense R.A. . . . . .Lt. Col. Field

```
8—Coast Defense R.A. . . . . . . . . . . . . . . .Lt. Col. Shaw
12     "     "     R.A. . . . . . . . . . . . . . .Lt. Col. Penfold
22 and 40 Coy. R.E. . . . . . . . . . . . . . . . .Col. Clifford
               R.A.S.C. . . . . . . . . . . . . .Col. Levenge
               R.A.O.C. . . . . . . . . . . . . .Col. Hopkins
               R.A.M.C. . . . . . . . . . . . . .Col. Simpson
               R.A.P.C. . . . . . . . . . . . . .Col. Ford
               R.A.V.C. . . . . . . . . . . . . .Major Simpson
               C.M.P. . . . . . . . . . . . . . .Major Kerr
Field Accounting Staff . . . . . . . . . . . . . .Col. Kilpatrick
               R.A.D.C. . . . . . . . . . . .Lt. Col. McCurdy
               A.E.C. . . . . . . . . . . . . .Major Wood
               R.C.S. . . . . . . . . . . . . .Lt. Col. Levett
H.K. Mule Corps . . . . . . . . . . . . . . . . .Major Stanfield
               R.A.F. . . . . . . . . . . . . .Wing Cmdr. Sullivan
               H.K.V.D.C. . . . . . . . . . . .Col. Rose
```

Canteen Prices and Some Increases in Prices*

Articles	1/12/43	22/2/44	22/8/44	28/11/44	31/12/44
Soya Bean Milk Powder	4.85	12.40	21.60	19.60	65.60
Rock Salt	1.90	2.60	2.80	4.00	19.80
Tausi Beans	—	3.30	7.60	7.00	12.20
Potatoes:					
Irish (lb.)	—	2.30	7.10	—	—
Sweet (lb.)	1.00	1.70	3.25	—	—
Golden Syrup (2 lb.)	6.05	19.00	22.00	52.50	82.00
Dried Beans (lb.)	—	8.00	14.70	22.00	42.00
Soya Sauce (12 oz.)	.95	4.20	7.70	13.20	—
Bean Curd	2.00	5.85	8.25	—	—
Local Jam (2-6 oz.)	2.60	7.95	12.65	18.10	—
Local Soap	.85	2.85	3.05	—	—
Matches	.30	1.10	2.10	2.10	4.00

* [All prices in Japanese yen.]

234

Pepper (per oz.)	.35	—	1.10	—	11.50
Tomatoes (large)	1.50	3.20	4.50	—	—
Vinegar (pt.)	—	—	12.75	—	63.00
Egg Yolk Powder	—	—	20.00	—	59.80

Feb. 14/45 Downtown Markets for Chinese New Year

Chicken per catty (1 ⅓ pounds)	240.00 yen
Duck " "	200.00 yen
Sausage meat " "	240.00 to 400.00 yen
Duck eggs (each)	16.00 yen

Monday, February 19, 1945

Dearest Molly and Harvelyn,

We are all hoping for Red Cross supplies very soon. About the end of January the paper told us that a Red Cross ship would sail from Japan to Hong Kong and other places. It was to leave Japan on the 17th of Feb. Lordy, how we need these supplies. Our diet is at the lowest ebb of all time. Even our rice has been cut and

235

when we finish a meal we could start all over again and eat twice as much if we had it to eat. Rice and vegetable tops sort of leave one pale after months of nothing else. I sold my watch and ring to buy a few extra things in the canteen, but now there isn't anything in the canteen to buy, except brown sugar at 34 yen per pound. . . . The 17th was Harry's birthday. He opened his last can of bully beef and the four of us had a darn good meal—Harry, Ernie, Jack and I. It gave us 3 oz. of meat each and how good it tasted. Ernie has one tin left. Jack and I have used ours in the same way. I opened mine for Harvelyn's birthday. The weather has been awful this month—cold, wet and windy—and we wear everything we own all day long, and sleep in or under everything we possess, and still nearly freeze. If we had some decent food our blood wouldn't be like water. Damn their hides!

Ken

Tuesday, February 27, 1945

A real surprise for us today. Cigarettes arrived from home, also some personal parcels. I received 4,000 cigarettes: 2,000 Sweet Caps and 2,000 British Consuls. Are they a treat. After smoking the stable sweepings that have been sold to us at over eight yen per ounce, these cigarettes are unbelievably good. Some of the

Canadians received about 25,000, and one or two none at all. We have heard there are four times as many parcels yet to come. I hope so, as I am looking forward to your parcels and the clothes in them. We as a camp are a damned ragged-looking bunch of humans—and I mean ragged. I have given about 1,000 cigs. and it does one's heart good to see them enjoy a real smoke. Mine came from the following: 1,000 Mutual Life, 2,000 from the Overseas League, 1,000 from ? as the sender's name had been lost in opening when they—the Japs—examined the boxes, so I don't know whether it was from you or not, Sweetheart. These cigs. were among the first lot to be shipped. Jack Bailie got a parcel from Eva. I remember him saying she had sent a parcel at the time of your letter of over two years ago [and had] mentioned yours being sent. So I am optimistic about eventually receiving yours.

Best love,
Ken

Saturday, March 3, 1945

We have just been given a Red Cross parcel, the English parcel like our first one received about two years ago. These parcels have been here all the time spoiling, and now as another Red Cross ship is in the harbour, they are handing these out. Just to think, after all these months of living on rice and little else they produce more parcels. They no doubt have enjoyed many of them. However, all this should be over soon and we won't think of anything but getting home to the ones we love.

Ken

Sunday evening, March 4, 1945

Harry, Ernie and I had a wonderful dinner at noon today: ½ lb. of bacon between us and a fried duck's egg each, and fried tomatoes with our rice. The bacon came from the Red Cross parcel (we received two yesterday), the tomatoes from our garden, and the duck's eggs, Santa Claus brought them at 20 yen each. And did we enjoy our meal. It was heavenly, I can tell you. We are now waiting for our tea to come up. I am going to have some jam, biscuits and cheese. Such affluence in eats is something we haven't experienced for many months. I had Nestlé's milk with my porridge this morning, it was lovely. You will never have any trouble feeding me ever. The tea is here so good-bye for now, Sweetheart.

Ken

Hello, Sweethearts,

I hope you are feeling like a million and that the weather is starting to improve. It is getting warmer and more livable here. Since our cigarettes arrived on Feb. 27, we have had duck eggs daily: we get four eggs for one packet of cigarettes (20's). Eggs are ¥20 each, so cigarettes are again the medium of exchange, and the addition of eggs to our diet has made life more cheerful. The yen is worth practically nothing. Our pay is ¥120 per month, which equals six eggs. Some lavish pay, what? Our Red Cross parcels are a godsend, and when we have them to work on we can spin our parcels out for quite a while. Ernie, Harry and I open one tin of something or other and divide it; in this way we will have something besides rice to live on. The Japs are giving us the barest minimum, the so and so's. We are all hoping that Germany will cave in one day soon, and that will hasten the show ending here, I hope.

Today's menu. Breakfast: porridge, Nestlé's milk, brown sugar. Lunch: a sort of bologna sausage and rice. I have put a few onions in my tin, also tomatoes. Supper: rice and greens, plus maybe an egg. Breakfast is now ready so good-bye, Dearest.

Ken

Hello, Sweethearts,

I notice it has been 12 days since I last wrote in this book. Absolutely nothing to write about. The weather is much warmer and we are no longer going around with all the clothes we possess on our backs day and night. Prices are still soaring. A packet of Canadian Black Cat cigarettes sells here for ¥120, the same amount of money as the Japs pay me each month. We have sold enough cigarettes to buy eggs with, and how we enjoy them. We can get eight duck eggs for ¥120, which again equals our princely salary. The Japs are still feeding us on rice and greens, so the eggs are really wonderful. Have had two each day for the past two weeks, and some days three. I will soon get fat on such sumptuous fare. The Nips are moving all internees from the island of HK to the mainland. They must be going to defend the island in case of attack and leave Kowloon an open city. I hope so. Am writing a card to you tomorrow.

Best love to you both,
Ken

Today is Easter. I have been thinking of you and Harvelyn all dressed up in your new Easter things and going to church. How I wanted to be with you. I went to early Communion at 8:15, just after our morning parade. We have had glorious weather for the past three months and all has been very quiet with only an occasional plane over, taking a look around. The news we get in the paper shows the Americans are really pouring it into the Japs, and the scrap in Europe looks so hopeful. I am expecting to hear it is all over any day. I hope I am right. I hope you have had a wonderful Easter, both of you, and that you had lots of fun hunting Easter eggs, Harvelyn. I had two duck eggs and they were darned good.

Best love to you both,

Ken

Tuesday, April 3, 1945

We have had two wonderful air raids, yesterday and today. And did the boys unload the bombs—our huts shook from the explosions of bombs that hit just over half a mile away, and some of them much nearer. I don't know how many B-29s there were in the raid, but they were up about 25,000 feet and they still looked large and glistened in the sunshine. Yesterday the alarm was on for over four hours and today nearly as long. They flew back and forth and simply plastered the docks and shipyards and gun positions. Hope they keep it up.

Best love,
Ken

Wednesday, April 4, 1945

We had another three-hour raid today. It was a pippin. We could see the B-29s, they were awfully high up and looked so large. With the sun shining on them they seemed to be made of polished silver. Yesterday during the raid one flight flew right over our camp. They released the bombs before they, the planes, reached our camp, and we could hear the whistling roar of the bombs as they came down, passing over our camp and smashing the docks about half a mile away, and setting things on fire. A good few pieces of shrapnel were picked up in the camp. This came from the anti-aircraft guns of the Japs.

Today's raid was simply terrific! I don't know how many planes there were, but they did some carpet bombing on the island and we can only see the top of the mountains; everything else is obscured by dense, black smoke from burning oil. I

242

think our hosts are somewhat perturbed over the attentions that are being showered upon them these days. I hope it keeps up until we are relieved. We can see several machine gun positions that are being built in the hills not far from our camp. They will, no doubt, be the cause of many deaths when this place is—if it ever is—attacked.

[K.]

Tuesday, May 1, 1945

Dearest,

It has been nearly one month since I have written in this book. The past two weeks have been fairly busy ones in spots. We had to move thousands of oil barrels the Japs had stored in huts in our barracks. Then we had to move into these huts, clean them and get *all* our things transferred. The biggest job was putting up a few shelves. Then last Sunday, 50 officers from the other camp moved into our lines, so we have all but six of the Canadian officers here now. It makes it ever so much nicer being together. In five of the huts, the Japs have stored merchandise brought from the downtown warehouses and put here for safety from looting. Only, about 10 of our guards broke in and looted a lot of things. They were arrested. One committed suicide, and two broke out of jail and got away. Our guards are from Formosa and aren't as truly Japanese as [the others] might be.

By the paper, Germany is about through, and Mussolini and his close followers have been killed. Japan seems to be catching it in the neck properly, and we are all jolly well fed up. Our meals are pretty awful these days: rice and ground bean porridge twice daily, three times a week, and today we had some boiled sea weed and it was, well, not up to much. I gave mine away and when I give food away in here, believe me, Zantippa, it isn't very palatable. I have just bought ¼ lb. of salt fish.* I cut them up, heads and all, and fry them and put the result with my rice. It helps get it down. Our monthly pay, 120 yen, will buy eight duck eggs or 1 ½ lbs. of dry beans or three pounds of salt and a number of other things that one can't live on for long. Oh, when I get home I am going to be at the refrigerator hourly, day and night.

[K.]

* My father had a drawing of one that is too faint to be reproduced. A salt fish is not quite the length of a thumb.—*Ed.*

Wednesday, May 9, 1945

Hello, Sweethearts,

I am sure you are all feeling very glad and thrilled to know that Germany has at last packed in. I am sure our "hosts" here must see the handwriting on the wall most clearly. Things here are in a pretty rotten state, and the value of the yen is steadily approaching the vanishing point. For instance, the tram fare of 10 cents Hong Kong before the war is now 20 yen and the Japs say the yen is worth five times the Chinese dollar or what used to cost 10 cents now costs 100. We haven't been paid yet this month and the reason given is that they haven't any paper to make out the paylists, but expect to do so in a few days. It will be wonderful to get something to eat but porridge, rice and greens. No meat or fish of any kind, unless we buy fish, and eggs are impossible to get enough of at 14.50 yen each. However, it shouldn't be much longer when we will be saying, "Well? That's over," and we will all be scrambling to get home. H-O-M-E. What a wonderful word, and the wealth of meaning contained in those four letters.

Best love,
Ken

Monday, May 14, 1945

Before breakfast. Nearly a week has passed since I last wrote you and nothing has happened but many rumours. I am sure there was great rejoicing when Germany finally folded up, but we seem so far away from all those things. To me China is a country entirely surrounded by barbed wire and, so far as I am concerned, the Chinese can have their darned country.

Harry and Ernie are both in hospital. Ernie has catarrhal jaundice* and Harry has malaria. One year ago, on the 11th of this month, we came over here from Argyle Prison Camp—and I went right into hospital that day with dysentery. Haven't been sick since but am keeping my fingers crossed. If we don't get some more food soon we all will be on the sick list. Just paid 30 yen for two eggs. Will have them for my supper tonight.

Best love,
Ken
(porridge has just arrived)

* Catarrhal jaundice is another term for hepatitis A.—*Ed*.

Hello Sweetheart,

We are in quarantine—our hut—28 of us. Harry Hook was taken to the hospital yesterday. He was terribly ill and this morning we were quarantined. He has spinal meningitis. Luckily we have in the hospital a new drug that is supposed to knock blue blazes out of the damn germ. Harry has responded to this drug wonderfully, but of course it is days too soon to know just how it will turn out. But it's too bad to have a thing like this happen when the end of the war seems so near. We are all so damned depressed.

Best love,
Ken

Monday, May 21, 1945

My Dearest,

Another anniversary of your birthday has rolled around. How I wish I could be with you to celebrate it in a fitting manner. However, I have put forward my best efforts and built a "cake." At least I will dignify my maiden effort by calling it that. It is about the size of a grapefruit and has all the characteristics of a rubber heel, but being a valiant soldier I am going to eat it and then wait patiently for the doctor or undertaker to arrive. After careful consideration, I might be doing the camp engineers a good turn if I bored a hole in it and fitted a handle, with the idea of making a sledge hammer of it. I am sure it would stand up to most any work it might be put to. I am sure you will have a wonderful birthday and hope you stage a good party or are at one. It will take me a long time to catch up on birthday presents, Christmas, etc., etc., for you and Harvelyn. I will be with you before many months have elapsed.

Yours,
Ken

Wednesday, May 23, 1945

Dearest Molly and Harvelyn,

It is cold and rainy. I have long trousers and a sweater on and [am] not too warm at that. We are still in quarantine and will be until the end of the month. Harry is slowly improving. He has been awfully ill and just by good fortune we had some of the necessary drug to kill that awful germ.

248

It seems I will never get to the end of patching. Of course nearly everything we have is in rags. My two suits of pyjamas have at least a dozen patches on them, and undershorts, shirts, etc., the same. I shudder to think what we will look like when we get out of here. On the other hand, I am sure we won't care one darn, we will be so elated to be free. We hear wonderful rumours of tremendous task forces gathering around Japan and I hope they are all true. Those little Bs have all the Allies can give coming to them and then some, for the many atrocities they have committed during this war. To read in the paper the mealy-mouthed utterances their premier makes in his speeches, you would think their whole nation was wallowing in the milk of human kindness. When John Chinaman gets at the Japs left in China after this show is over, it will be one great massacre. There will be very few of them to ever see Japan again and this is no idle utterance.

I made my second cake yesterday. It wasn't as nice as the first, so you can imagine how bad it was. However, I will make another tomorrow and put an egg in it. At 16 yen each it makes a cake *costly*. We are told that our rations will be cut again on the first of the month, but we can yet live a long time, if only on hope.

Tomorrow being the 24th, a holiday, I suppose Harvelyn will be having a great time with her friends. I had hoped so much to be home by the end of June this year so we could all have a good holiday together after school finished, but we will have to postpone it for a little longer. Best love to you both.

Ever yours,
Ken

Sunday, June 17, 1945

Dearest Molly and Harvelyn,

Time does slide by. It doesn't seem three weeks since I last wrote to you in this scrap-book. Harry is still very seriously sick. He has had two bouts of malarial fever since he was taken ill with meningitis, as though that wasn't enough to kill most people. Then three days ago he had a relapse and the meningitis started showing up again. They give him spinal injections, which are pretty bad in themselves, and the treatment he is given is most strenuous. They make him so sick to his stomach, he can't keep anything down. He has about a 50/50 chance I am told.

"Meat" came in again yesterday for the third time, only some dirty Bs cut off 100 pounds of the best and only left us 150 pounds, mostly bones. I don't know who is responsible for this meat, but surely the Japs could watch their supply depot more closely than that. I hope they make it up next week. It is awfully hot, 95 degrees, and the bed bugs are here in millions. Lordy, how I hate them. I go over my bed several times each week and get hundreds. They drop from the roof and everyone is in the same boat. Isn't this a cheerful pageful?

The Japs have stopped our paper so we don't get any news. We had a raid about one week ago. Hong Kong was bombed with incendiary bombs. And from the smoke we saw, there must have been one mile of the city on fire.

There is a plane that comes over nearly every day, taking pictures I suppose. We call him Hank. Why, I don't know. He must be up about 25,000 feet but he flies back and forth covering the whole area. He isn't just doing it for fun. I wish we could get some really late news. It would cheer us up no end. We can't be far from the finish now, but time does drag. I wrote another letter, which is supposed to be sent by radio. I don't expect it will be, as they have more urgent and important things to do in trying to win a lost fight.

They brought a number of parcels the other day of men that went to Japan. They were divided among the whole camp. I got a pair of heavy woollen socks and a tin of tooth powder. The powder tastes so good, after using what has been supplied for tooth powder.

For about a year and a half they have been holding back some of our pay. Now they want us to sign a receipt and let them use the money they call "interest for prisoners of war." Whose prisoners or what prisoners isn't made quite clear. We in our hut have voted not to sign. We could use the 500 or 600 yen they have deducted to buy a little to eat, but at that it wouldn't go very far: beans, ¥120 per pound; onions, ¥50 per pound; sugar, ¥75 per pound; rock salt, dirty as the devil, ¥20 per pound; tobacco, ¥36 per oz.; cigarettes, ¥25 for 20. So you can see our pay of 120 yen per month doesn't go very far. Everyone has sold all their personal effects long ago for eggs, etc. Eggs now are 25 yen each. Isn't it a lovely place to live in?

Best love,
Ken

Monday, June 25, 1945

Dearest Molly and Harvelyn,

Another week has gone by and what heat we are having. The thermometer doesn't seem to know how to go below 90 degrees day or night, so we simply stew day and night. Harry is in very bad shape; his heart has gone "phut." Jack Crawford told me this morning one valve is very badly punctured so it will more than likely be curtains for him. Harry has been a darn good soldier and officer, and in my opinion the best in the Canadian force out here. It is a shame this has had to happen at this late date. We all feel very gloomy over it. I wish I had a very large box of candy or chocolates right now. I crave something sweet, and as brown sugar is 80 yen per pound, we just don't buy it at all. In fact we can't buy anything at the present prices, except onions at 50 yen and an occasional smoke, but another few months should see the end of this internment or the end of us. Everyone is losing weight very rapidly and we can't stand it forever.

Ken

Friday, June 29, 1945

Dearest Molly and Harvelyn,

Today being the sixth birthday I have been away from home since the war started, I think it is about time it should cease. Have been thinking of you both all day and I know you both have been thinking of me. [There is] one thing I have resolved to do after eating what is jokingly called our noon meal. I am installing an extra stove, fully equipped, in our kitchen at home and will be busy between meals getting something to eat, because I am sure that one stove couldn't stand the strain of producing enough food to satisfy me.

Rice and greens for lunch, plain rice for supper, and porridge for breakfast, all without one damn thing to make them taste better—if that would be possible. One thing: I have quite a sylph-like figure. Harvelyn wouldn't have a chance to tease me about my tummy. However, by the time I reach home, providing the food is good on board ship, it might just be slightly convex instead of very concave.

They took Harry to the hospital over near our old prison camp at Argyle. I don't think he will live for very long. He has put up an awful fight, but his heart has all gone to pieces and he weighs about 90 pounds. I hope they will be able to make things easier for him over there. The hospital here is like a barn with a roof that leaks like a screen door. After every rain the place is flooded. After reading this over, it sounds pretty blue. I guess it is seeing Harry off that does it.

Best love to you both,

Ken

Saturday, July 14, 1945

Dearest Molly,

This is the 1,322nd day of our captivity. Never before did I realize just how long it takes to pass that many days. We do get so fed up with nothing to do and less to eat, and are forever in a squabble with the Japs over shortages in wood, rice and everything else that we are supposed to receive as prisoners of war—mail, parcels, cigs., etc. Consequently, we have to sell anything we may have to buy such things as may be procurable to eat. Yesterday I sold my sterling silver table fork and two sterling silver spoons for ¥257.40. That is more than two months' pay. I got beans at ¥112.00 per pound; wheat bran, ¥47.00 per pound; and rock salt at ¥25.40 per pound, and still have some money left. Sugar is ¥148 per pound so we don't have sugar. They say it costs 200 yen to send a letter from Hong Kong to Canton—80 miles—and 400 yen to send one anywhere in the interior of China. Of course, we are blockaded and nothing much is coming in. However, we can stand it, and are looking forward to the final scrap when we will be released. Must go on parade now.

Best love,
Ken

Wednesday, July 25, 1945

Dearest Molly,

It has been over 10 days since I attempted to scribble in this book and since then we have heard of Harry's death. He was taken to the hospital near our old prison camp at Argyle St. on my birthday, June 29, and died on the seventh of July. He put up a marvellous fight against odds that were too much for anyone to cope with. His heart was badly infected and finally gave out. One gets to know a chap pretty well under circumstances such as we have been living during the past three years and a half. He was a damn good officer and soldier, the best in the force that came out here and to think that now it is nearly over, to have to pass on. I hope his heart will find all the things he desired and liked on the other side.

I am writing this in hospital. Have been here nearly one week. Malaria. My first bout. I don't like it either. A mosquito must have sneaked up behind me when I wasn't looking and nipped me. There is a lot of malaria here. I have been lucky, haven't been in hospital since a year ago last May. Am getting nicotinic acid injections for pellagra. My mouth, tongue and face around lips and nose are darned sore. Then I just caught a sneezy cold so am doing right well by myself.

Love,
Ken

256

Dearest Molly,

 Just one week since I last took my pencil in hand and wrote in this scrapbook. Have been feeling sort of rotten. Malaria, plus a heavy cold on my lungs, resulting in a lot of congestion. Has pulled me down to a new all-time low in weight for I imagine the last 40 years. I got weighed this morning—125. I seem all knees and elbows. I have been taking for two weeks now 30 grains of quinine and 30 grains of sulphapyridine a day, so you can imagine just what it does to my appetite. It has almost reached the vanishing point. I try like everything to get as much food as possible down, but it doesn't amount to much. However, today is my last day of the sulpha dope and my appetite should return with a bound. I have a figure like a lath, straight up and down. Of course, I don't expect you to believe me, or Harvelyn either, but there is a complete absence of paunch, in fact a marked depression. Everyone is as cheerful as can be. It just can't last much longer—or can it? We are pretty fed up and all looking forward to getting some food when this is all over. We have been on half-rations for over a week, porridge twice a day and greens at noon, and everyone has lost weight to beat the band. Cheerio for now.

 Best love to you both and will I be glad to get home and see you,

 Ken

Monday, August 6, 1945

Sweethearts,

All this week, or for nearly 10 days, it has simply rained cats and dogs. I have been in the hospital for the past 29 days. Came in with malaria and then took bronchitis. The building leaks like a screen door. On the fourth we had a visit from the Red Cross representative, Mr. Lyndle. He just walks through and never says one word. The Japs have the stage all set for him and only allow him to go where they want. Consequently, he never sees the squalor we really live in. Believe me, it is far from what the world is lead to believe. Well, rice is just being served. Our supper is rice only, about seven tablespoons full. Bye for now.

[K.]

Wednesday, August 15, 1945

Holy swill barrels, "Katy," are the rumours rampant. For the past five days, the Chinese outside have been telling the men that go out on working parties the war is over, and that a truce of a few days has been arranged and that we will be relieved in a few days' time. Some men have become actually ill and taken to hospital from excitement. It doesn't take much, after three years of sickness and continuous shortage of food and other essentials, to throw a person's digestion out of balance. The rumours keep coming in daily and the vernacular papers say so many conflicting things that most of us are just sitting back waiting. We are convinced the war is over; I hope we are right.

Everything around the harbour and all activities that we are able to observe have suddenly ceased. The sentries who guard us are feverishly buying anything in the clothes line and paying huge amounts in military yen—practically worthless—for things; also charging fantastic prices for the few "comforts"—*really bare necessities*—they bring in. We are hoping for some Red Cross things one day soon. Of course, we don't know whether they have any for us or not, but there should be piles of stores and parcels. We have only had seven in the last three and a half years, and lots of things that used to come through our canteen looked suspiciously like R.C. goods. Prices are really amazing. For instance, bananas, darn poor ones too, are 150 yen for one and a third pounds. That is 30 yen more than they pay us per month. Matches (five-cent safety matches at home) are ¥21; beans, ¥250 per pound; bran, ¥90 per pound; tea, ¥125 per pound; wheat, ¥150 per pound (the quality would be no. 5 musty or feed wheat); sugar, ¥625 per pound; rice, over ¥600 per catty . . . best cigs., ¥34 per ounce, etc., etc., all the way down the line. It is funny to see a sentry with the seat out of his pants pulling a wad of 100 yen notes out of his shirt that amounts to thousands of yen and paying 200 yen for a pair of black cotton socks and a singlet that would cost 35 cents bought in Woolworth's.

We all have sold nearly everything but the bare necessities to buy food with. Yesterday I sold a pair of slacks I had made in camp here out of wind breakers two and a half years ago, and an old pair of khaki shorts that had been altered, with some tar on the seat of them and a hole in them, too, for 550 yen and half a box of matches. I bought beans and other things and some smokes and have about 250 left. It's really ludicrous.

However, it will soon be over now. I have made a cake today. Being a very modest chap as far as my cooking abilities go, I can only say that the hardiest dog would more than likely be doubled up with indigestion if he ate one of them. However, we dig into them and say "Not bad" simply because we have to put something into the old paunch to keep from looking too much like those pictures we all have seen of natives of India when food was really scarce in their home towns.

We had two little pigs. Last night they squealed their last, and at noon today we had a stew. They also put six hens in it too. The hens apparently went on a sit-down strike and wouldn't lay, so now they are just a memory.

Best love for now, Sweetheart,

Ken

Yesterday was a day that we have been waiting for for such a long time. We had been receiving illicit news through Chinese papers smuggled into camp, also from men coming in from work parties. Finally Col. White sent for the Jap camp commander and demanded to know just why we hadn't been officially informed the war was over. We finally were sent the official [Imperial] Rescript of the Emperor. Then we knew for sure it was all over. I can't begin to write my feelings. After all these years behind barbed and electrified wires and living on food that, to say the least, has been awful—and then thinking of all those that were killed, or have died—it is just impossible to write how one feels.

Today I have been busy trying to make my raggy clothes look less ragged, and it is just impossible to appear as a well-dressed officer. We will, no doubt, be issued with new outfits. God knows we need them. Tomorrow we are supposed to be released, so rumour has it. So you will, I am sure, understand why this will be a disjointed entry. We haven't been very emotional or demonstrative as yet. Maybe when we are actually relieved we will give vent to feelings that at present don't seem to want to be expressed in a hilarious way. Oh Sweetheart, when I think that we should be together very soon now, I nearly go mad with joy. Won't it be glorious when we three are together again.

Bye-bye for now,
Ken

Monday, August 20, 1945

Dearest Molly and Harvelyn,

For the last five days we have been in an awful dither. Rumours and pseudo-authentic reports have been coming in by the hundreds and still those darn little brown apes are temporizing. The Japs and the guards have all faded into the background and we have been sending out the odd truck trying to get food. The Japs sent in a little tinned milk for our hospital patients, and sugar and oil. I don't know whether I mentioned it or not, but the first thing to arrive in the way of supplies, sent in two days before any food stuffs, was a large shipment of *Scott tissue*. No! they haven't any sense of humour, but thank God we have.

Yesterday was a wonderful day for the Hong Kong Volunteers officers and men. Their wives and families were allowed to come and see them. It was both wonderful and pathetic, and the stories of atrocities and terrible treatment are really awful.

One man bound to an iron bed and fire built under it until he was dead, treatment of women too awful to write down—damn their souls to hell! I hope the Americans show them no mercy, and they should be exterminated as a nation. Yesterday afternoon our band played and the wives and families danced and had a great time.

How I thanked God that you two are in a country where you can be and act natural, and not have to walk along the street with your eyes on the ground, not daring to speak to any friend you may meet. Of course we are impatient and pretty well all at a high nervous tension, but we would smack anyone that accused us of it. Dozens have gone to hospital with their stomachs all awry and running temperatures. Purely nerves. None of us are eating much, and sitting up late, and smoking too much, but then one only has an experience like this once in a lifetime unless they are most unlucky. For the last two nights we have had electric lights, the first in over a year. Summer and winter we have had to sit in the dark, and believe me it gets on one's nerves at times.

Yesterday we were issued with ¾ lb. of sugar. I made an alleged cake and put nearly half a pound of sugar in it. The result was sweet. After being without sweet things for months, one doesn't miss it so much, but every once in a while one gets a hankering for it, so I have had my fling at sugar for a few days.

A number of officers left for Fort Stanley [nine miles away] to see their wives and families. . . . [They had been separated since the invasion and have had mail service] only three or four times a year. They have several British NCOs who have been working with the Japs under arrest. One is accused of burning most of the mail we have been writing home for the last year or more. Well, I must stop now. More later.

Best love,

Ken

Wednesday, August 29, 1945

Visited Stanley Jail. Will tell you all about it later.

[K.]

Thursday, August 30, 1945

HK Relief Fleet:

2 aircraft carriers
HMS *Indomitable* (Rear Admiral Harcourt)
HMS *Venerable*

Battleship: *Anson* (Rear Admiral Daniels)
2 cruisers: *Swiftsure*, *Euryalus*
6 destroyers: *Kempenfelt*, *Ursa*, *Whirlwind*, *Quadrant*, *Toscin*, *Pyrias*
Submarine depot ship: *Maidstone*
8 submarines
Minesweepers (Australian)
HMCS [*Prince*] *Robert* (Can. ship)
Hospital ship: *Oxfordshire*
Transports included *Empress of Australia*

   This afternoon Rear Admiral Harcourt came into camp and gave us a little talk
and looked around. Were we glad to see him and his staff. But before he came a
number of reporters and cameramen from our own Royal Canadian Navy ship,
the *Prince Robert*, came into camp and took some pictures. I was in two of them.
Oh, Molly, you have no idea how wonderful it was to see some honest-to-God
white people. They all seemed so big, fat and healthy; it made us all look and feel
frightfully scrawny and grubby. I had a wonderful time talking to them. In the
evening we went by parties down to the dock and went on board. I had a couple
of drinks of rye whisky and certainly felt the good of it. We all have been on the

"Interdict List" for 44 months and some of the boys certainly were feeling very sorry for themselves for a while. However, it did everyone a world of good, and we stayed up until after 2:00 a.m. chattering like a bunch of school-girls. Ernie and I are going down again this afternoon to have a look around. The city is in an awful mess, and the whole city will have to be rebuilt, it seems to me. The Chinese are looting every chance they get. It shouldn't be long now. We are told we are going to Manila first, then home. I hope we arrive by the 27th of September, Dearest. Wouldn't it be just too wonderful if we could celebrate our 23rd anniversary together? Oh boy! I find one can only get excited up to a point, and if one should go beyond that—well, the atomic bomb would be a mild explosion to what we would cause. We are getting so much to eat these days—meat, stews, vegs., etc. Not such quantities that our appetites seem to have vanished, but we are doing all right. All this sounds very incoherent, so will stop and try later. Best love, Sweetheart.

To an early reunion,
Ken

Winnipeg Free Press

VOL. 51—No. 294—22 PAGES.   Sun rises 6.51, sets 20.00.   WINNIPEG, FRIDAY, SEPTEMBER 7, 1945   Forecast—FAIR, COOL.
Moon rises 7.44, sets 20.54.

600 CANADIAN PRISONERS RECOVERED

Friday, September 11, 1945

Dearest Daddy,

This is the first real letter I've been able to write you and it seems so funny to be able to use as many words as I want. It's marvellous to think that we will be seeing you in two or three weeks. Mum and I are both well. I was in Vancouver this summer and was staying with Katy Farris. I was with her for seven weeks and had a perfectly wonderful time. We were at Bowen Island for 10 days. I rode horseback and went fishing. I caught a 3 ½ lb. rock cod one day when I was alone. Very ugly, but I had a good meal from him. Later we went over to Victoria by boat for the day. We *flew* back (Katy & I). Katy was teaching me to drive her car and I was getting along nicely. I've grown a lot since you last saw me. I'm about 5'6" now—taller than Mum. When I got home I found my room had been painted a pale pink and my bed was painted. Mum and I painted my bookcase cream so it all looks very nice. We are saving our ration coupons so you will have a nice big roast (etc.) to come home to.

Mum is starting to get cupboards and a drawer ready for you and your *new* clothes. So many people have been phoning us and writing letters. There will be a line-up of your friends a mile long to see you. I will have to have tickets printed and sell [them] at a dollar each to look at you, Daddy Dear. I wish so much that I could meet you in Vancouver but I guess I can't. We are expecting a cable from you in the near future. Try and bring home a Japanese medal or something. I am at R.H. Smith school this year in Gr. 9. It's my last year there, but I don't know where I will be going next year.

Lots of love and be seeing you soon,
Harvelyn

Appendix

**DEPARTMENTS OF NATIONAL DEFENCE
ARMY**

July 5, 1946

Dear Major Baird:

Its task so splendidly fulfilled, the Canadian Army is now being demobilized and accordingly, it has become possible for you to retire from active service and return to your civilian status.

This personal note will convey to you the sincere appreciation of the Minister of National Defence and of the Army Council for the services rendered by you to Canada as a member of her Armed Forces. Your association with the Army and your contribution to its success should always be a matter of justifiable pride to you.

May I take this opportunity of wishing you good health and every success in the future.

Yours very truly,
(E.G. Weeks)
Major-General,
Adjutant-General.

"The Queen and I bid you a very warm welcome home.

Though all the great trials and sufferings which you have endured at the hands of the Japanese you and your comrades have borne resistantly in our thoughts. We realize from the accounts which we have already received how heavy those sufferings have been. We know too that these have been endured by you with the highest courage.

We mourn with you the deaths of so many of your gallant comrades.

We hope with all our hearts that your return from captivity will bring you and your families a full measure of happiness."

George R.I.

Message from King George VI, December 1945.

271

A SUMMARY OF APPROXIMATE CASUALTIES.

Officers.

Unit or Formation.	Killed or Died of Wounds.	Missing.	Wounded.	Total Strength.
H.Q. China Command	2	2	3	33
H.Q. R.A.	—	1	—	6
8 Coast Regt. R.A.	—	—	3	19
12 Coast Regt. R.A.	1	1	1	16
5 A.A. Regt. R.A.	—	8	1	23
1 Hong Kong Regt. H.K.S.R.A.	3	7	3	24
965 Def. Bty. R.A.	—	—	1	3
22 Field Coy. R.E.	—	1	—	7
40 Field Coy. R.E.	2	—	—	7
R.E. Services	—	1	1	18
2 Royal Scots	12	4	11	35
1 Middlesex Regt.	10	2	4	36
Canadian Staff	2	4	3	14
Winnipeg Grenadiers	6	8	12	42
Royal Rifles of Canada	6	8	4	41
5/7 Rajput Regt.	6	4	7	17
2/14 Punjab Regt.	3	—	5	15
Royal Corps of Signals	1	—	—	7
R.A.O.C.	3	2	1	15
R.A.S.C.	2	—	3	24
R.A.V.C.	—	—	—	2
R.A.M.C.	2	1	—	28
Royal Army Dental Corps	—	—	—	4
R.A.P.C.	—	—	—	5
Hong Kong Mule Corps	—	—	1	3
Indian Medical Services	—	1	—	5
H.K.V.D.C.	13	6	13	89
	74	61	77	538

Total battle casualties 212   39·5 per cent.

List of casualties, published in the
Supplement to The London Gazette, *Tuesday, January 27, 1948.*

Unit or Formation.	Killed or Died of Wounds.	Missing.	Wounded.	Total Strength.
8 Coast Regt. R.A.	19	2	23	285
12 Coast Regt. R.A.	15	2	24	200
5 A.A. Regt. R.A.	16	11	10	231
1 Hong Kong Regt. H.K.S.R.A.	2	2	10	30
965 Def. Bty. R.A.	2	4	8	58
22 Field Coy. R.E.	8	20	9	213
40 Field Coy. R.E.	2	7	1	220
R.E. Services	2	5	1	54
2 Royal Scots	96	45	188	734
1 Middlesex Regt.	94	25	110	728
Canadian Staff	6	10	5	78
Winnipeg Grenadiers	28	222	60	869
Royal Rifles of Canada	42	157	160	963
Royal Corps of Signals	16	5	14	177
R.A.O.C.	13	26	4	117
R.A.S.C.	23	10	11	183
R.A.V.C.	2	—	—	3
R.A.M.C.	13	3	3	146
Royal Army Dental Corps	—	—	2	6
R.A.P.C.	—	—	—	25
Military Provost Staff Corps	—	1	—	3
Corps of Military Police...	—	—	—	18
Army Education Corps	—	—	—	8
H.K.V.D.C.	196	139	135	1,296
	595	696	778	6,645

Total battle casualties 2,069   31 per cent.

Unit or Formation.	Killed or Died of Wounds.	Missing.	Wounded.	Total Strength.
8 Coast Regt. R.A.	—	1	4	233
12 Coast Regt. R.A.	3	—	3	187
5 A.A. Regt. R.A.	24	80	15	332
1 Hong Kong Regt. H.K.S.R.A.	144	45	103	830
965 Def. Bty. R.A.	2	—	4	86
5/7 Rajput Regt.	150	109	186	875
2/14 Punjab Regt.	52	69	156	932
R.I.A.S.C.	—	—	1	13
Hong Kong Mule Corps	1	5	5	250
I.M.D. and I.H.C.	—	2	—	55
	376	311	477	3,893

Total battle casualties 1,164   30 per cent.

1. All figures are approximate as accurate information can only be obtained when the Casualty Bureau has all facts and figures.

2. The wounded does not include lightly, or returned for duty, wounded. The total wounded shown is 1,332 but A.D.M.S. states that 2,000 wounded men passed through our hospitals alone, and many of the wounded of the 5/7 Rajput Regt. fell into Japanese hands and have not been recorded.

The final figures will probably be approximately :—

	Killed or Died of Wounds.	Missing.	Wounded.
Imperial Officers	74	61	
Imperial Other Ranks	595	696	
Indian Other Ranks	376	311	
	1,045	1,068	2,300

3. It has been impossible to collect any reliable data regarding the casualties suffered by the 450 locally enlisted Chinese.

4. Regarding Japanese casualties.

A local paper reported a Memorial Service held at Kai Tak Aerodrome to 1,995 Japanese who fell in the attack on Hong Kong. That figure is certain to be an under rather than an over statement.

A Japanese Medical Major told me early in January 1942, when I was appealing for assistance for my sick and wounded, that he had 9,000 wounded on his hands in Kowloon and on the Island.

Taking the wounded figure to be correct, and remembering that many must have been drowned on the assault on the Island, the averages of the last war should give about 3,000 and NOT 1,995 killed.

The Japanese admitted in broadcasts and in conversation to me that they had suffered severe casualties. The Chinese have stated that 10,000 were killed, but this is undoubtedly an oriental exaggeration.

True figures will never be known, but from the above a fair estimate can be made :—

Killed	3,000
Wounded	9,000
Total	12,000

And many of the latter died of their wounds, for funeral pyres near their hospitals were observed regularly for some months.

Major K.G. Baird, CIC
Suite 1A, Bebary Apartments
Winnipeg, Manitoba

OTTAWA, *December 22, 1951*

Major Kenneth G. Baird
Ste. 1A, Debary Apartments
Winnipeg, Manitoba

Dear Sir:

I beg to inform you that the recent careful review of your case showed an increase in your disability from coronary sclerosis resulting in acute myocardial infarction. Your disability from this condition, bronchitis, traumatic arthritis of your left knee and avitaminosis† with residual effects has now been assessed at 100 per cent.

It is considered that you have no assessable degree of disability from gunshot wound of your right ear resulting in chronic catarrhal otitis media, pyorrhoea and dental caries.*

† Avitaminosis is a generic term for diseases, such as beriberi and pellagra, which result from a shortage of vitamins.—*Ed*.
* Catarrhal otitis medea is a chronic infection of the ear. Pyorrhea, resulting in the loosening of the teeth and their possible loss, is an inflammation of the gums.—*Ed*.

275

I am again attaching a treatment leaflet; you still have full treatment rights for your service-related conditions.

Your pension, therefore, is being adjusted at the increased rate of 100 per cent.

The Chief Treasury Officer will send you a statement of your account. I am sure you will readily understand that a little time must elapse between the writing of this letter and the adjustment of your account by the Chief Treasury Officer.

Yours faithfully,
LOH/GB.
Superannuation No. W 8 1 3 9 1
OTTAWA, Ontario

Major K. G. Baird 2 Wars Veteran, Dies At Home

MAJOR K. G. BAIRD

Major Kenneth George Baird, veteran of two wars, died Wednesday at his home, 1A Debary apartments, 626 Wardlaw avenue. Major Baird served with the 44th battalion during World War I with the Winnipeg Greneaiers in World War II and was a prisoner in Hong Kong.

He was with Aetna & Son Life Insurance Co. and later with the Unemployment Insurance Commission in Winnipeg, retiring in 1955. He was a member of Fort Rouge branch of the Canadian Legion.

Surviving are his wife, the former May Havelyn Dowling, a daughter Mrs. Fraser McInnis; two sisters, Mrs. Gordon Thorpe and Mrs. Helen Hebert; and two brothers, A. W. and R. Baird. Funeral service will be at 1:30 p.m. Friday in St. Luke's Anglican church, Rev. J. C. Clough officiating. Burial will be in military plot, Brookside cemetery. A. B. Gardiner funeral home is in charge.

Honary pallbearers will be W. L. Billings, W. J. Hunter, J. R. McMillan, H. Adamson, F. F. Tribe, R. W. Payne and W. McPhillips. Active pallbearers will be Lt. Col. George Trist, Lt. Col. J. A. Bailie, Capt. Neil O. Bardal, Capt. F. V. Dennis, Lt. R. W. Queen-Hughes and Capt. Hugh McKechnie.

Winnipeg Free Press, May 10th 1957.

July 24, 1957

Mrs. May H. Baird
Suite 1A, Debary Apt.
626 Wardlaw Ave.
Winnipeg, Manitoba

Dear Madam,

As the widow of the late Kenneth G. Baird, a contributor under the Public Service Superannuation Act, you have become entitled to an annual allowance. We are enclosing herewith cheque No. A9-J072285 in the amount of $22.49 in payment of this allowance as indicated below:

(N.B. Only these statements indicated apply in your case.)

Your allowance is payable at the rate of $12.91 per month during your lifetime or until remarriage. Enclosed cheque covers the period from May 8, 1957 to June 30, 1957.

Enclosed is a brochure containing information which might be of interest to you as the widow of a civil servant. It is suggested you retain it for future reference.

Future payments will be made by cheque direct from this Department on or about the last day of each month. Kindly advise the Chief Treasury Officer, Finance Building, Tunney's Pasture, Holland Avenue, Ottawa, attention Mr. Lahey, of any change in your permanent address.

Yours truly,
D.E. Anderson
Chief, Superannuation Branch

DEPARTMENT OF VETERANS AFFAIRS
Ottawa 4, Ontario

September 19, 1957

DVA (WSR 3)
Mrs. May H. Baird
Suite 1-A, Debary Apartments
626 Wardlaw Avenue
Winnipeg 13, Manitoba

Re: Major Kenneth George BAIRD, V.D.

Dear Madam:

Information has now been received from the Canadian Pension Commission that the death of your husband, Major Baird, was attributable to his military service.

As your husband's death was related to service, a silver Memorial Cross awarded by the Canadian Government as a slight token of appreciation of the sacrifice you have made, will be prepared and forwarded to you by registered mail.

Yours truly,
H.M. Jackson

280

Acknowledgments

To my agent Kathryn Mulders, who believed, and made me believe, after ten years of trying, that this could really happen. My very grateful thanks for a wonderful experience.

To Don Loney, my editor at HarperCollins, and to all the staff who were so kind, knowledgeable, encouraging and so young, for guiding me through so patiently, my thanks.

To my friend, Jacqueline Mulders, who typed the entire manuscript, for someone who never learned to type!

To James Kostelniuk who was so helpful in locating pictures, and to Lynn Crothers of the Winnipeg Free Press Archives, who spent hours helping me to locate and identify their dates.

To Cliff Chadderton of the War Amps who wrote the foreword.

To Judith Lafontaine of the Hong Kong Commemorative Association in Winnipeg, who rounded up some of the excellent pictures in this book. My thanks.

And last, but not least, to the Red Cross, whose parcels were the difference between life and death.

This book has been truly serendipitous.

The faculty of making fortunate discoveries by accident.

My thanks,

Harvelyn